D1627184

Jossey-Bass
Pfeiffer

The Art and Science
of Competency Models

Anntoinette D. Lucia

Richard Lepsinger

The Art and Science of Competency Models

Pinpointing Critical Success Factors in Organizations

JOSSEY-BASS/PFEIFFER
A Wiley Imprint
www.pfeiffer.com

Copyright © 1999 by John Wiley & Sons, Inc. All rights reserved.

Published by Jossey-Bass/Pfeiffer
A Wiley Imprint
989 Market Street, San Francisco, CA 94103-1741   www.pfeiffer.com

ISBN: 0-7879-4602-8

No part of this publication may be reproduced, stored in a retrieval system, or transmitted in any form or by any means, electronic, mechanical, photocopying, recording, scanning, or otherwise, except as permitted under Section 107 or 108 of the 1976 United States Copyright Act, without either the prior written permission of the Publisher, or authorization through payment of the appropriate per-copy fee to the Copyright Clearance Center, Inc., 222 Rosewood Drive, Danvers, MA 01923, (978) 750-8400, fax (978) 750-4470, or on the web at www.copyright.com. Requests to the Publisher for permission should be addressed to the Permissions Department, John Wiley & Sons, Inc., 111 River Street, Hoboken, NJ 07030, (201) 748-6011, fax (201) 748-6008, e-mail: permcoordinator@wiley.com.

Jossey-Bass/Pfeiffer books and products are available through most bookstores. To contact Jossey-Bass/Pfeiffer directly call our Customer Care Department within the U.S. at (800) 956-7739, outside the U.S. at (317) 572-3986 or fax (317) 572-4002.

Jossey-Bass/Pfeiffer also publishes its books in a variety of electronic formats. Some content that appears in print may not be available in electronic books.

Library of Congress Cataloging-in-Publication Data

Lucia, Anntoinette D., date.
     The art and science of competency models: pinpointing critical success factors in organizations / Anntoinette D. Lucia, Richard Lepsinger.
         p. cm.
     Includes bibliographical references (p.   ) and index.
     ISBN 0-7879-4602-8 (acid-free paper)
     1. Employees—Rating of.   2. Personnel management.
3. Organizational effectiveness.   I. Lepsinger, Richard, date.
II. Title.   III. Title: Pinpointing critical success factors in organizations.
     HF5549.5.R3   L82   1999
     658.3—dc21   99-6326

Printed in the United States of America

Printing   10   9   8   7   6   5

Acquiring Editor: Matthew Holt

Director of Development: Kathleen Dolan Davies

Developmental Editor: Susan Rachmeler

Senior Production Editor: Pamela Berkman

Manufacturing Manager: Becky Carreño

Jacket Design: Mark Ong

Contents

To my family, and especially Al, for their
never-ending love and support.
—A.D.L.

To my wife, Bonnie, who helps me see the possibilities in life,
and whose love and support give me the courage to go after them.
—R.L.

List of Exhibits

Preface

Competency models that identify the skills, knowledge, and characteristics needed to perform a job have been in use for more than three decades. In the last five years, interest in them and their potential to help staffing and development efforts has increased dramatically among our client group. We believe this interest will continue to grow over the next few years due to three key, related trends—intensified competition, aggressive cost management and downsizing, and the proliferation of 360-degree feedback systems.

In the superheated struggle for competitive advantage, many companies have focused on people as the key to success. Competency models are highly useful in ensuring that employees are doing the right things; clarifying and articulating what is required for effective performance, such models help organizations align internal behaviors and skills with the strategic direction of the company as a whole.

Competition has also made it imperative for many companies to become "lean and mean" if they are to survive. But as they take aggressive action to manage costs and slim down operations, they realize that reengineering and various other process improvements are not in and of themselves sufficient for competitive success. To maintain the same or higher productivity with fewer people, those who remain must have the needed skills and knowledge. More than ever, competency models help human resource and line managers decide about selection and placement, succession planning, and training and development; they are a means of ensuring that the organization's investment in people yields the expected results.

360-degree feedback technology is especially important in development, appraisal, and compensation systems. But if it is to be meaningful, it must focus on the skills and knowledge most relevant to the job and on the differences between more and less effective leaders and managers. If such feedback is to measure the critical skills and behaviors necessary for success, a precise definition of them must be made. That's where competency models enter in.

The development and use of competency models is seen by some as arcane: a discipline solely in the domain of academics and social scientists. Many books and articles over the last three decades have been targeted at academic, research, and social science communities. Consequently, their prevailing tone is formal and full of technical jargon and statistics. We see this as an opportunity to fill the gap with a practical "how-to" work that clearly and simply explains how to develop and use competency models.

We believe that this book makes a contribution to current knowledge and practice in three ways. As a result of our work developing competency models for a range of organizations and positions, we have streamlined and simplified the process. We have also developed practical approaches and processes that a business's internal resources can use successfully without the help of professionals who have a degree in statistics or other outside consultants. In addition, the book can serve as a single source for basic information about the development and use of competency models. Most of what is currently available focuses either on a specific study or a small component of the overall process, or else is so full of jargon and equations that it is overwhelming for the average reader.

We attempted to integrate information from various academic and real-life sources and present it in terms meaningful to our three intended audiences. The first is human resource professionals who are just beginning to look at competency models as a means to address the business needs of their organizations, and who require answers to many basic questions before they can use the technology successfully.

The second audience is more experienced human resource professionals who would like a comprehensive, nontechnical reference work on competency models that enables them to gain access to the information they seek without having to skim through dozens of magazine and journal articles and textbooks.

The third group is line managers who want to determine whether competency models can be genuinely useful for helping them address their business needs; having heard about the value of competency models from "experts" in the field, they now want to see for themselves just what all the fuss is about and to make an informed decision about how to proceed. These managers need the information to assess what is required to make the investment in competency models pay off and to determine if the costs are in line with the benefits.

The information contained in this book is derived from three sources. An extensive review of the existing literature and research provides an historical perspective and the insights of some of the best thinkers in the field. Our major contribution is to summarize the critical points and learnings of these researchers and social scientists and present them in language that is easy to understand.

We also base much of the book's content on our own practical experience and the insights we have gained from working with a range of clients over the years. As consultants, we have developed and implemented competency models for dozens of jobs and roles in a wide variety of organizations including Chase, Northwestern Mutual Life, Continental Grain, the New York Stock Exchange, Zeneca Pharmaceuticals, Geon, and Household International. Based on this experience, we present an approach to developing competency models that is readily usable by human resource professionals who have not had any specialized training in this area. We also share the lessons we have learned along the way that help ensure that a competency model initiative produces the intended results.

The third source of information is the first-hand experiences of consultants, human resource professionals, and line managers who have developed and used competency models in their own organizations. We include accounts of the obstacles they have encountered, the successes they have had, and the practical lessons they have learned along the way.

The book has seven chapters. In Chapter One, "The What, Why, and How of Competency Models," we define what a competency model is, describe its components, and discuss some of their broad, general applications. The chapter also includes a summary of the various methods of developing a competency model as well as an overview of the history and evolution of the technology.

Chapter Two, "How Competency Models Can Enhance Human Resource Management Systems," examines how competency models can be applied within selection, training and development, appraisal, and succession planning systems to support an organization's business objectives. We present case studies to illustrate how organizations have used competency models to maximize productivity, align human resource systems, enhance training and development and selection systems, achieve business strategy, and support large-scale organizational change. These case studies, and the accounts of practitioners' experiences, highlight what the reader needs to know and do to make certain that the competency model initiative achieves its intended objectives.

Chapter Three, "Competency Models: Laying the Groundwork," lays out a planning process that will help you to determine the objectives and scope of your project and to ensure the most efficient use possible of the time and resources you have available. Two approaches to developing competency models are presented: starting from scratch, and using an existing, validated competency model as a foundation and customizing it. A method for anticipating potential problems and minimizing risk during the model's development are also covered. Finally, we discuss establishing the performance criteria with which your organization measures success to better focus your data collection and analysis.

In Chapter Four, "Developing a Competency Model from Scratch," we describe specific action steps to follow during the development of the competency model from scratch. We discuss various methods of data collection and how they can be used to increase the likelihood of identifying the knowledge, skills, and characteristics required to succeed in the job. We also review, step by step, a method for data analysis that makes converting raw data into a competency model—that accurately reflects the relevant behaviors for effective performance—a clear and straightforward task. Finally, we review pitfalls to avoid during the development of the competency model and our recommendations to ensure these potential problems do not derail your project.

Chapter Five, "Finalizing and Validating Competency Models," discusses the steps to ensure that the competencies and associated behaviors described by the model are both relevant to the targeted job or role and validated as predictors of successful performance. We offer techniques to solicit feedback on the model from a larger cross section of individuals than the pool initially interviewed during the data collection phase. We also provide a scientifically rigorous method for establishing a correlation between the identified behaviors and those of successful performers in the job or role. These steps will increase your confidence when developing or enhancing human resource decision-making tools based on the model's content. Finally, we review the steps for developing competency models from the foundation of existing validated models and provide shortcut alternatives to both methods of competency model development for those organizations with time or resource constraints.

Chapter Six, "Integrating Competency Models into Human Resource Management Systems," describes the process of creating competency-based selection, training and development, appraisal, and succession planning systems. We discuss the methods for converting the model into the necessary formats or tools to integrate the competencies into each step of human resource management.

Chapter Seven, "Communicating Purpose and Gaining Commitment: Selling the Idea to Others in Your Organization," will help you use your knowledge of competency models and their development to win the support of others in your organization. We present a systematic plan for selling the idea to key decision makers whose commitment will be vital to your success. We cover the most frequently raised objections to the use of competency models and suggest how to respond. We also introduce a practical stakeholder analysis model to help you determine the level of support you can expect from key individuals and groups, the reason for their lack of commitment, and ideas to overcome resistance. Guidelines and checklists are provided that outline how to develop a communication plan and how to gain the cooperation and commitment of key stakeholders.

Acknowledgments

As with our first book, *The Art and Science of 360° Feedback* (1997), writing *The Art and Science of Competency Models* was as much a process of learning as it was a process of documenting our ideas and experiences. It was gratifying to use conversations and feedback to help test our thinking, shape our message, and present our ideas.

We are grateful to many people for their help and support during the writing of this book. In particular we would like to thank

- Our clients, including those not specifically cited in the text, who willingly shared their experiences with competency models.

- The practitioners and professional associates whose contributions ranged from a critique of our initial ideas to a detailed description of their work and experiences with the development and use of competency models—particularly Mark Baca, Dwight Coffin, Mark Edwards, Andrea Eisenberg, Jeanne Gruner, Robert Joy, Sue Keenan, Lyle Maryniak, and Carol Schmidt.

- The reviewers who took the time to read our rough drafts and give us tremendously useful feedback and suggestions: Ann J. Ewen, Gail Howard, Karin Kolodziejski, Penny Nieroth, Scott Parry, Bernie Rosenbaum, William Rothwell, Meg Salter, and Harold Scharlatt—with special thanks to Bev Christie for her work above and beyond the call of duty, and to Shannon Wall for her breakthrough suggestions.

- Our colleagues at Manus, for their support and assistance on this project and on many of our other projects that were affected by this work: Dave Bilas, Marie Boccuzzi, Debra Carbonaro, Janet Castricum, Jeff Cicone, Howard Cohen, Cecile Derisson, Pat Doherty, Debbie Horne, Terri Lowe, Sid Nachman, Jennifer Owler, Kristy Sammis, Ian Shearson, Laurie Tubbs, and Kim Verbert. Special recognition to JT Rehill for his dedication to this project, and special thanks to Steve Wall—we couldn't ask for a better partner.

- The staff of Jossey-Bass/Pfeiffer for their professional and thoughtful support throughout this endeavor.

- Evelyn Toynton, Jessica Rae, and Bliss Broyard, whose assistance during the editing process enabled us once again to produce a reader-friendly text that makes our ideas more accessible, and whose energy and attention to deadlines kept us on schedule.

- Our friends and family members, for their support and patience. In particular we would like to thank our spouses, Allyn Keiser and Bonnie Uslianer, who put up with our late nights, early Saturdays, and extended work weeks as we attempted to meet our deadlines. We promise not to take on another book project for at least three years.

Finally, we thank you, the reader, for choosing this book as a resource for yourself and your organization. We hope you enjoy reading it and that it proves to be an informative and useful resource.

April 1999   ANNTOINETTE D. (TONI) LUCIA
Stamford, Connecticut   RICHARD (RICK) LEPSINGER

The Art and Science
of Competency Models

Chapter One

The What, Why, and How
of Competency Models

In today's global and fiercely competitive business world, state-of-the-art technology, superior products, and a steady source of capital are tickets of entry into the marketplace. Many organizations find that the key to gaining a competitive edge is the ability of their workforce to maximize these advantages. Put simply, a company's technological tools are only as useful as its employees' ability to employ them; the perceived value of a product is determined in part by how effectively its benefits are communicated (McLagan, 1989).

An organization may find, however, that determining whether its people possess the abilities critical for its success is difficult. The behaviors necessary for effective performance vary from one business to another and within organizations from one role to another. Thus many companies have begun using competency models to help them identify the essential skills, knowledge, and personal characteristics needed for successful performance in a job and to ensure that human resource systems focus on developing them.

To better understand the benefits of a competency-based human resource management (HRM) system, picture this scenario: you are able to hire people who have high potential to succeed, to ensure that they receive the training and development necessary to realize that potential, and to provide an appraisal system that gives them the feedback and coaching they need to perform well. Imagine also being able to focus on the skills, knowledge, and characteristics employees need and to ensure that they understand what it takes to move up or over in the organization. And finally, envision being able to demonstrate that the behaviors and skills you identify and develop are proven predictors of success. How can you do all this? By identifying the traits that contribute to the success of the organization's top performers.

Let's take a look at how one company used a competency model to address its business need. A mortgage banking company's successful launch of its paperless mortgage (featuring little or no documentation needed to apply for a mortgage) was met aggressively by competitors. To respond, the company realized it had to develop its sales force. It needed to rapidly increase the number of sales associates in the field, but doing so was challenging because of its unique products and the fierce competition in the industry for talented sales-people. Also, it needed to address high turnover in field offices and wide variance in sales effectiveness among those offices. On closer look, the company determined that regional managers, who hired people and managed the sales force day to day, did not have a clear picture of what was required to do the job. Frequently, the criteria used in hiring decisions—a candidate's previous experience or a manager's intuition that the person "had what it takes"—did not address the specific job requirements. The company's solution was to develop a sales competency model (Exhibit 1.1) that clarified the characteristics required to succeed in the job.

The competency model was used in two ways. First, it was integrated into the company's selection system to make sure that everyone involved in the hiring decision was working from the same criteria shown to be related to effective performance. Second, the model was incorporated into the performance management system to ensure that salespeople would receive coaching and feedback on the behaviors and skills that had the strongest correlation to success on the job. As a result, newly hired sales associates were able to get up to full productivity faster, and turnover also decreased.

A Closer Look at Competency Models

The American Heritage dictionary defines a competency as "the state or quality of being properly or well qualified." That is a good general description, but it does not clarify what is being measured

Exhibit 1.1 Sales Competency Model for an Associate in a Mortgage Banking Company

Ability

Mental agility

Ability to deal with multiple issues and details; alertness; learning capacity

Quantitative reasoning

Ability to reason with, analyze, and draw conclusions from numbers; feeling comfortable with quantitative data

Divergent thinking

Ability to see and think beyond the obvious and formulate original solutions

Personality

High emotional stamina

Ability to maintain focus and effectiveness under stressful and frustrating situations

Assertiveness

Ability to take command of face-to-face situations while displaying appropriate tact and diplomacy

Self-sufficiency

Ability to maintain one's motivation and work independently for extended periods of time with minimal support and approval

Sociability

Desire to interact with others; projecting warmth; relating to a wide variety of people

Competitiveness

Desire to win and to achieve and surpass goals; persistence in the face of obstacles

High energy level

Ability to establish and maintain a fast pace and tempo

Exhibit 1.1 Sales Competency Model for an Associate in a Mortgage Banking Company, cont'd.

Skills

Basic selling skills

Establishing rapport, determining customer needs, relating benefits to product features, handling objectives, and closing

Problem-solving skills

Anticipating problems, inviting ideas, distinguishing symptoms from causes, modifying proposals, and implementing solutions

Presentation skills

Ability to communicate to large and small groups, establish rapport with the group, articulate delivery of ideas, read group cues, effectively use visual aids, and maintain a commanding presence

Coaching/training skills

Assessing learning needs and closing knowledge gaps, simplifying information, ensuring understanding, reinforcing desired behavior, and motivating the learner

Knowledge

Financial analysis

Understanding the financial impact of decisions on the customer, the customer's customer, and the company

Computer literacy

Basic computer skills for application to marketing programs, including prospect lists, customer contacts, and relevant economic data

Product knowledge

Expertise related to the company's product and services, as well as other crucial aspects of the business

Competitive environment

Knowledge of competitive forces and how the company stacks up against competitors and their products and evaluated by organizations that are so intent on assessing their employees' competencies nowadays.

A more relevant definition, widely accepted among human resource specialists in corporate environments, is "an underlying characteristic of a person which results in effective and/or superior performance on the job" (Klemp, 1980, p. 21). A more detailed definition, synthesized from the suggestions of several hundred experts in human resources development who attended a conference on the subject of competencies in Johannesburg in 1995, is "a cluster of related knowledge, skills, and attitudes that affects a major part of one's job (a role or responsibility), that correlates with performance on the job, that can be measured against well-accepted standards, and that can be improved via training and development" (Parry, 1996, p. 50).

A competency model describes the particular combination of knowledge, skills, and characteristics needed to effectively perform a role in an organization and is used as a human resource tool for selection, training and development, appraisal, and succession planning. Although this might seem fairly straightforward, the more we consider what is entailed in identifying and measuring these competencies, the more complexities are revealed. Skills, for example, can range from highly concrete proficiencies, like the ability to operate a particular machine or to write a sentence that clearly presents an idea, to far less tangible capabilities, such as the ability to think strategically or to influence others. Obviously any job requires a mixture of skills that may seem more or less measurable depending on their degree of concreteness. For example, devising a test to determine whether someone can type quickly and accurately enough to be a valuable member of a word-processing team is relatively easy. It is trickier to determine whether someone is skilled enough at strategic thinking and influencing others to be an effective manager.

Knowledge, too, can be either highly tangible and measurable— do you know the proper pressure setting during the blending stage of product production?—or a far more complex matter: do you understand the workings of the Brazilian financial market and how it is likely to be affected by various global developments?

But of all the components involved, the characteristics of a person are probably the most complex and least readily measurable. A personal characteristic can be an aptitude, innate talent, or inclination that suggests a potential to acquire or use a particular kind of skill or knowledge. For example, a mathematical aptitude demonstrates a potential for acquiring accounting skills. Other examples include a mechanical ability, a talent for logic, or an innate affinity for highly detailed work. Characteristics can also describe a personality trait that demonstrates a particular way of relating to the external environment. Personality traits such as self-confidence, self-sufficiency, or emotional stability may indicate a disposition for dealing with certain types of situations and performing certain kinds of roles or functions. For example, self-sufficiency may suggest success in working independently with little supervision.

Obviously, aptitude and basic personality traits are, to a certain extent, innate in an individual; you cannot teach an aptitude for mechanical things the way you can teach a particular rote skill. Still, someone with an aptitude for mechanical things is more able to master a mechanical process, just as someone with an aptitude for languages will be quicker to master Portuguese. But, as the second definition of competencies cited earlier indicates, a growing body of opinion says that even traits that might seem to be innate "can be modified and developed" (Zemke and Kramlinger, 1982, p. 29). Furthermore, even personality traits that might appear non-quantifiable—charisma, for example—can be measured and assessed when they are translated into behavioral terms.

At our consulting firm, Manus, a Right Management Consultants company, we believe that a competency model should include both innate and acquired abilities. It is essentially a pyramid (see Exhibit 1.2) built on the foundation of inherent talents and incorporating the types of skills and knowledge that can be acquired through learning, effort, and experience. At the top of the pyramid is a specific set of behaviors that are the manifestation of all the innate and acquired abilities discussed earlier.

Exhibit 1.2 Competency Pyramid

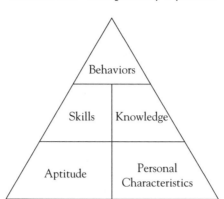

Expressing these abilities in behavioral terms is important for two reasons. First, for a competency model to be useful as a human resource tool, it must not only define the competencies necessary for effective performance but provide examples to illustrate when a particular competency is being demonstrated in a job. In the mortgage banking company model, for example, the definition of problem-solving skills (anticipating problems, inviting ideas, distinguishing symptoms from causes, modifying proposals, and implementing solutions) provides the regional manager with the specific criteria to assess a sales associate's performance. Second, although innate characteristics are fixed in a person for the most part, behaviors can be modified and taught. In other words, it might be difficult (some would say impossible) for a person lacking empathy to develop that trait, but empathetic behaviors, such as listening to customers' needs or addressing their concerns, can be fostered through training and development.

Therefore, our data collection process for the development of competency models—which may consist of interviews, questionnaires, focus groups, or a combination—focuses on concrete, specific behaviors that can be taught or altered through training, coaching, and other developmental approaches. Similarly, the model itself is couched in behavioral terms. This approach also facilitates the validation component of a competency model study. We encourage the observation of outstanding performers when feasible to validate that the behaviors contained in the model accurately describe the way these individuals carry out their work.

Depending on their objectives, our clients have defined the scope of their competency models in various ways. Some models are meant to identify the core competencies that are relevant and necessary to all members of an organization, no matter what their level or role. Note that the term "core competencies" as used here refers to behaviors illustrated by all levels of the workforce rather than a business's unique strengths as they are sometimes understood. For example, reflecting particular business objectives, a core competency of customer focus must be demonstrated by an entry-level customer service representative (answering a telephone call by the third ring, using polite language, and the like) as well as a regional manager (resolving customer problems by coordinating cross-organizational resources, analyzing buying patterns to ensure availability of products, and the like). Other models are intended to pinpoint the competencies required for effectiveness in a given unit, type of job (such as manager or consultant), or position (such as plant manager or market analyst). At their most sophisticated, such competency models take into account the particular nature of the external and internal environment in which the person must operate, the type of client or customer with which the person must deal, and any other job-specific factors that could require a special set of competencies for effective performance.

If you are thinking about developing competency models, keep the following points in mind. Although certain competencies, such as customer focus or problem-solving skills, might be generic across several organizations, the behaviors relating to those competencies can still vary widely from one company to another, just as they may vary from one role or job or level in a company to another. For example, the behaviors involved in successfully selling cars may differ from those required to successfully sell pharmaceuticals (although the abilities and personality traits might be the same). Within the same organization, two management jobs may present very different challenges and require very different skills. For a competency model to be as useful as possible, it should be developed with a specific role in mind. For that reason, even the best off-the-shelf "generic" competency model, based on very high-quality research, will be more effective if it has been customized.

What Business Needs Can Competency Models Address?

Clarifying Job and Work Expectations

When we ask people in seminars what is wrong with traditional HRM systems, the most frequent response is a lack of agreement on performance expectations and measures. Many people lament that critical human resource decisions appear arbitrary, that they are not based on an objective set of criteria that is generally accepted within the organization. This is true whether we are discussing selection, training and development, appraisal, or succession planning.

A competency model addresses this concern directly by answering two questions: What skills, knowledge, and characteristics are required to do the job? What behaviors have the most direct impact on performance and success in the job?

In selection systems, a competency model ensures that all interviewers are looking for the same set of abilities and characteristics. In training and development and appraisal systems, the model provides a list of behaviors and skills that must be developed to maintain satisfactory levels of performance. For succession planning, competency models ensure not only that decision makers focus on the same set of attributes and skills but that these are important and relevant to success in the positions under consideration.

By clarifying performance expectations, competency models also serve the interests of individuals. Specific job requirements provide a clear understanding of what is expected of them, and targeted training and development can enhance their personal development. Appraisal systems focused on the use of specific behaviors and practices offer people a road map for recognition, reward, and possible advancement.

For companies with a global presence, competency models help ensure that consistent standards are applied worldwide. For example, at New York–based Colgate-Palmolive, competencies are tied to performance appraisal, development planning, and a 360-degree feedback system. Robert Joy, senior vice president of Global Human Resources, explains that the competencies "allow [the company] to have a consistent, simple approach to managing across the globe. We need to manage human resource functions like an equity. For example, the person who manages Colgate Toothpaste globally makes sure it stands for the same thing around the world. The packaging, formula, advertising, the position against our competitors on pricing are all the same. To improve the overall capability of our organization, we manage our people and the required competencies for successful performance the same way" (personal communication, December, 1998).

A shared understanding between an organization's leaders and its associates about how to perform the work and what it takes to succeed helps to increase the likelihood of higher retention rates, job satisfaction, and the achievement of strategic goals.

Hiring the Best Available People

In today's competitive job market, where it is getting harder and costing more to find the right people, organizations want to ensure that human resource dollars are well spent. Competency models are seen as a highly useful tool to make sure that human resource systems facilitate and support a company's strategic objectives.

By clarifying what specific behaviors and practices make for employee effectiveness, competency models increase the likelihood that hiring costs such as the use of recruitment firms and signing bonuses contribute to placing the right people into the right jobs.

At Colgate, the human resource department teamed up with individual business units throughout the world to create competency guidelines for every job function. Based on these guidelines, a set of interview questions was developed to identify whether candidates possess the necessary skill sets for effective performance. Robert Joy of Colgate explains that his company tracks the success of the competency-based selection process by looking at the number of high-potential employees in each business unit: "We track our global high potentials. For example, if we've hired X number of people, we track them on the basis of how well they're performing. At the decision level, we look at succession planning to see how many of the people we have hired fall into the high-potential box" (McIlvaine, 1998, pp. 18–20). According to Joy, the process has succeeded in helping the organization locate top talent worldwide.

Maximizing Productivity

The superheated competitive climate of the global economy has made it imperative for many companies to become "lean and mean" in order to survive. As organizations take aggressive steps to manage costs, they realize that reengineering and various other process improvements are not in and of themselves sufficient to ensure competitiveness. Rollins and Fruge (1992) describe how ARCO Transportation approached this. To maintain the same or higher productivity, it is essential that people have the specific skills, knowledge, and characteristics required to be effective. By identifying relevant skills gaps, competency models help ensure that training and development dollars will be spent wisely—for example, on programs and development experiences targeted to teach crucial skills and behaviors. Competency models also allow for the development of appraisal systems that evaluate people on their use of behaviors and practices that directly contribute to competitiveness, encouraging both the business and the individual to focus on whatever will have the greatest impact. As seen in the example of the mortgage banking company, competency models can help focus selection, training, and evaluation systems on the necessary competencies to ensure maximum productivity.

Enhancing the 360-Degree Feedback Process

Over the last ten years there has been increased use among Fortune 500 companies of 360-degree feedback for development, appraisal, and compensation purposes. The 360-degree feedback process involves collecting perceptions about a person's behavior and its impact from the person's boss or bosses, direct reports, colleagues, fellow members of project teams, internal and external customers, and suppliers to form a comprehensive portrait of behavior on the job. The "reality check" offered by the process makes it a popular training and evaluation tool in many organizations.

The 360-degree feedback process is useful for describing how people actually carry out their work, but it is made more meaningful when focused on the behaviors necessary to perform the job most effectively. Competency models help ensure that such feedback relates specifically to the competencies crucial to individual and organizational success.

When Zeneca Pharmaceuticals decided to implement a feedback instrument as a development tool for managers, a number of existing, off-the-shelf instruments were evaluated. While all had their strengths, none measured managers on the same behaviors included in the competency framework Zeneca had adopted several years prior as part of its performance management system. Since the competency model already described behaviors designed to help people and the organization achieve high performance, and employees were already being held accountable for the behaviors via the performance evaluation process, it made sense to align the evaluation tool with the same behaviors. Thus, they reviewed all of the performance management system's competencies and, from them, created a subset of behaviors deemed critical for success as a manager within Zeneca Pharmaceuticals; they used this subset as the basis for the feedback instrument. The resulting tool allows managers to receive feedback from their direct reports on criteria relevant and important to the organization and uses a common language understood by the company as a whole.

Adapting to Change

In this era of rapid change, the nature of people's jobs is often in flux, and new skills may increasingly be required to take on changing roles in the organization. Competency models provide a tool for determining exactly what skills are required to meet the different needs of today and the probable needs of the future.

Take the example of one life insurance company, whose general agents were responsible for managing the overall operations of the agency. With increased competition in the industry, a changing marketplace, and changing needs of both clients and agents, the general agents were being asked to focus more on strategic marketing, territory development, and building leadership teams. The company was concerned that the people they were selecting to fill the general agent roles might not all be equipped to meet the arising challenges of the changing business environment. By using a competency model to determine what behaviors the general agents were now required to perform, the company realized that the job was very different from what it had been five years earlier. In addition to possessing the traditional and still critical competencies used for recruiting and developing agents, the general agent was now expected to focus more intensely on thinking strategically and leading more complex agencies. Consequently, the company could begin to adjust its selection criteria to reflect the changing demands of the role. It could also determine what kinds of training current general agents needed by identifying their skill gaps and deciding which of these gaps ought to be addressed immediately to ensure continuing high performance.

Aligning Behavior with Organizational Strategies and Values

A competency model can be an effective way of communicating to the workforce the values of senior management and what people should focus on in their own performance. For example, competency-based appraisal systems help distinguish individuals with the characteristics required to build and maintain an organization's values (teamwork, respect for the individual, innovation, or initiative, for example) from those who do not exhibit the behaviors that will support these values day to day. In this way, competency models can translate general messages about needed strategy and culture change into specifics.

Pfizer's corporate finance division is an example of an organization that has effectively defined competencies to help create the kind of organizational culture it believes necessary to be the best in its class. "Within our Finance group the Pfizer competency model serves as the cornerstone for all key management activities," said Gregory J. Vahle, vice president of employee resources and services. "These activities include training and development, recruiting and selection, coaching and counseling, succession planning, reward and recognition, and our performance management systems." Several years ago, the finance division developed a competency model that has been implemented throughout the organization. More recently, it has undertaken a massive effort to clarify the core values that drive the company worldwide. Now, each of the business units and functional groups has begun to ensure that the two models work together to deliver a consistent message. For example, Pfizer's Corporate Finance Division has developed a 360-degree feedback process to provide people with information about how well they are using the leadership, managerial, and technical competencies relevant to their jobs. To reinforce the company's values, the feedback report lines up the behavioral items against the necessary competencies and organizational values. In this way, people can see how their behavior supports the company's values, and they get an overall picture of their use of key competencies. Individual development plans that address improvement in specific behaviors are also clearly linked to building and sustaining the organization's culture.

One of our global consumer products clients understands the role of a competency model in supporting the achievement of business strategy. It treats its senior management competency model as a strategic initiative. It is a strictly confidential document that must be handled in the same way any proprietary business information is handled. This organization correctly believes that if senior management competencies got into the hands of competitors, it would provide them with knowledge of its plans for development of senior managers and the strategy of the organization.

Who Invented the Competency Model?

In the early 1970s, a high-ranking official with the United States Information Agency (USIA) attended a workshop given by Harvard professor David C. McClelland, a distinguished psychologist with a particular interest in motivation and achievement. McClelland had developed a set of personality tests to identify which attitudes and habits were shared and demonstrated by high achievers.

It occurred to the USIA official that McClelland's approach might help to solve a persistent problem with the agency's selection procedures: although blacks and other minorities regularly applied for jobs in USIA libraries and cultural missions abroad, the agency's initial screening procedures almost invariably wound up eliminating them at the preliminary stages of the selection process. In addition, the tests proved to have very little relation to how well USIA officers actually did their jobs. The officer who approached McClelland presented him with a challenge: Could he identify the attitudes and habits of an outstanding USIA officer so that the agency could begin selecting employees on the basis of more relevant criteria than the screening tests?

McClelland said yes. He began by asking the USIA's personnel director and some top managers for the names of their most outstanding employees. He also asked for the names of people whose jobs were secure but who were in no way outstanding. To find out the difference between the two groups, McClelland and his colleague Charles Dailey initiated a series of intensive interviews with every name on their lists. They asked fifty people to describe three incidents where they felt they had performed outstandingly and three where they felt they had really messed up. McClelland and Dailey asked minutely detailed questions to establish a clear picture of what was said, what was done, when and where it all happened, who else was

there, and so on. These detailed descriptions enabled them, when analyzing the stories, to find a pattern: what competencies the outstanding performers had demonstrated that the others hadn't.

Some favorable competencies were far beyond the straightforward management skills that might have been expected. McClelland
explained to *New York Times* science reporter Daniel Goleman:

> One of the competencies was social sensitivity. A typical problem
> that cultural-affairs officers get into overseas is that there are direc-
> tives from Washington saying, for example, that you must show such
> and such a film. Now, if they're in, say, North Africa, they know
> damn well that if you show that film the place will be burned down
> the next day. A Washington politician thinks it's great, but the lo-
> cals will find it offensive. What they have to figure out, then, is how
> to show the film so that they can tell Washington that they did and
> yet not offend anyone in the country.
>
> The water walkers (i.e., star performers) came up with the solu-
> tion of screening it when nobody could come. In other words, they
> had the social sensitivity to know how the people in the country
> would react and also knew how to handle it back home.
>
> This example also points to another competence we have iden-
> tified: political judgment. It's a sort of political savvy that working in
> a bureaucracy demands. You have to be able to maneuver within a set
> of regulations and directives, balancing what the home office requires
> and what the reality in the field will allow. You've got to know what
> you can do and what you can't get away with. [Goleman, 1981, p. 36]

Interestingly, many of the skills that the panel of experts had identified as crucial to job performance turned out to be irrelevant to the
everyday duties of the people interviewed by McClelland and Dailey.

To validate his conclusions about which competencies were
necessary, McClelland tested them on another group of officers who
had been identified as outstanding and a group who fell into the
mediocre category. Using psychological tests that had been developed to assess an individual's degree of social sensitivity, as well as
tests for other key competencies, he and Dailey found that the offi-

cers identified as outstanding consistently performed very well on such tests, whereas those rated mediocre performed poorly. Thus it became clear that social sensitivity and the other key competencies they had identified were indeed relevant to job performance.

In 1973, McClelland wrote about hiring practices for civil service jobs. He pointed out the incongruity of using standardized psychological and intelligence tests, such as IQ tests and the Minnesota Multiphasic Personality Inventory, for certain jobs. How necessary is it, he asked, for a prospective policeman to be able to spot the correct definition of the word "lexicon"? Does anyone really believe that a talent for finding analogies to words will make someone a good firefighter? Yet the tests for civil service positions were typically composed of such items. McClelland argued for the use of competency testing in place of standardized tests. As he put it: "If you want to test who will be a good policeman, go find out what a policeman does. Follow him around, make a list of his activities, and sample from that list in screening applicants" (McClelland, 1973, pp. 1–14).

The same recommendation, of course, could have applied to corporations' use of standardized tests, which were then designed to predict academic performance rather than performance on the job. In fact, McClelland had chaired a panel of the Social Science Research Council that found that less academically successful students were not necessarily poorer performers in life.

Like most good ideas, McClelland's recommendations were not wholly new. As far back as the 1920s, Frederick Taylor, the father of scientific management, argued that the task of the management scientist was to break down the subject into its component parts— into competencies, in other words (Raelin and Cooledge, 1996, p. 25). And during World War II, psychologist John Flanagan developed what he called the critical incident interview, which attempted to identify crucial traits and skills required for successful performance by gathering data on the behavior and observations of people in relevant situations, such as job events, crises, key problems, and the like (Flanagan, 1954, pp. 327–358).

Unlike McClelland's approach, however, the critical incident technique did not pay attention to the interviewee's thinking patterns or feelings. It confined itself primarily to behavior that was generated and witnessed by the interviewee and other items deemed significant. But the behavioral approach McClelland used on the USIA project, which later became a key step in the process of developing competency models, expanded the focus to include individual experiences and perceptions of events.

From Theory to Practice: Translating Competency Models into Action

In 1973, McClelland and fellow psychologist David Berlew founded the company McBer to put his ideas on competency testing into practice. Since that time, the use of competency models has become increasingly widespread. In the past decade alone, thousands of organizations throughout the world have commissioned competency studies that are used as the basis for decisions about hiring, training, promotion, and other human resource issues.

Many different methods of developing competency models have evolved, but the most effective ones share certain characteristics. All of them follow McClelland's dictate to determine what leads to superior performance and to identify top performers and find out what they do. This can be broken down to two important principles: first, focus on highly successful people without making assumptions about their role, and second, pay attention to what they actually do.

The methods listed next are current development practices for competency models. The final outcome of them all is essentially the same: identification of behaviors required to successfully perform a given role. The difference is in how you get there.

- The *Job Competence Assessment Method* uses interviews and observation of outstanding and average performers to determine the competencies that differentiate between them in critical incidents (Dubois, 1993, pp. 72–84). See Spencer and Spencer (1993) for an extensive description of their research using this methodology.

- The *Modified Job Competence Assessment Method* also identifies such behavioral differences, but to reduce costs, interviewees provide a written account of critical incidents (DuBois, 1993, pp. 85–86).

- When using the *Generic Model Overlay Method*, organizations purchase an off-the-shelf generic competency model for a specific role or function (pp. 86–90).

- With the *Customized Generic Model Method*, organizations use a tentative list of competencies identified internally to aid in their selection of a generic model and then validate it with the input of outstanding and average performers (pp. 91–95).

- The *Flexible Job Competency Model Method* seeks to identify the competencies that will be required to perform effectively under different conditions in the future (pp. 98–107).

- The *Systems Method* demands reflecting not only on what exemplary performers do now, or what they do overall, but also behaviors that may be important in the future (Linkage, Inc., 1997).

- The *Accelerated Competency Systems Method* places the focus on the competencies that specifically support the production of output, such as an organization's products, services, or information (Linkage, Inc., 1997).

The approach to competency modeling we describe in this book builds on the thinking and work that have come before. As you can see, there are several approaches with solid underpinnings from which to choose. We believe that the process used to develop a model must be straightforward and easy to implement. The final product must have immediate, practical application and the commitment and buy-in of those who will be expected to implement or change their behavior based on it. Our approach also stresses the validation of competency models. That is, the development process should include a step to ensure that the behaviors described in the model correlate with effectiveness on the job. How you proceed depends on your objectives, your resources, and your situation.

A detailed description of our approach, which we also recommend to our clients who are planning to develop competency models internally, is offered in Chapters Four and Five.

Concluding Remarks

To decide whether competency models might help your organization achieve its goals, ask yourself the following questions:

- Are you recruiting and hiring people with the skills your company needs now and in the future?
- Once you have hired the best, most qualified candidates you can find, are they able to carry out their assigned jobs in the organization? Are development experiences available to help them perform at their highest potential?
- Are people recognized and rewarded for behaviors that specifically support established business goals?
- If a cultural or strategic change is under way, do people understand what they need to do to support it? Is there general consensus on behaviors required to ensure the organization's success?
- If there are plans to use a 360-degree feedback process, is it clear what behaviors people need to perform their jobs effectively and what behaviors they should desire feedback on? Is there a well-understood relationship between the use of these behaviors and the achievement of business goals?

If you answered no to any of these questions, you are not unusual. Few organizations are thoroughly prepared for the future or currently have all the systems in place to make optimum selection, development, training, and succession planning decisions. Nor is it uncommon for culture change or a switch in strategic direction to be a source of employee confusion.

In the next chapter, we look at examples of companies that have used competency models to achieve their strategic business goals as well as the specific ways that competency models can enhance human resource systems.

Chapter Two

How Competency Models
Can Enhance HRM Systems

Competency models are increasingly being used as the foundation of human resource management systems (McLagan, 1997). In the last chapter, we looked at some of the business needs that competency models can address. Now we examine how they can be applied within selection, training and development, appraisal, and succession planning systems to support these business objectives. The case studies in the second half of this chapter demonstrate how a broad spectrum of companies used competency models to achieve a variety of strategic goals.

Competency models can play a vital role in every process of HRM systems (Briscoe, 1996). By identifying the competencies necessary to be effective in a job, an organization can focus its selection, training and development, performance appraisal, and succession planning systems on the behaviors that have the most relevance to successful performance. Although the continuity that competency models can bring to HRM systems would certainly benefit an organization, many choose to introduce models into their systems gradually. Enhancing or modifying a selection or training and development system based on the results of a competency model study may meet with easier approval from management than attempting to apply the model to appraisal and succession planning. Factors such as the organization's culture, the business need that is being addressed, and the commitment of key decision makers may help to determine where to begin using a competency model in your HRM systems.

Understanding the value of competency models to various HRM systems will help you judge how best to apply them in your organization. It will also help you determine the scope of your project as well as the key stakeholders whose support is required for it to succeed. Exhibit 2.1 summarizes the benefits of using competency models for each HRM system. Chapter Six focuses on specific steps for implementing competency models with various human resource systems.

Benefits of Using a Competency-Based Selection System

Although competency-based selection systems have been around for many years, they have recently gained in popularity. Tight labor markets and the need at many organizations to squeeze more output from a shrinking workforce make the initial selection decision critical from a cost and productivity perspective. High turnover and lengthy adjustment periods while new hires reach full performance capacity quickly erode an organization's ability to compete. Many senior executives see selection as a significant means of differentiating their organizations—through people who provide excellent customer service, product development, or leadership, for example—and as a cornerstone for building and maintaining highly competitive and effective cultures. Following are ways that competency models can benefit the selection process.

Provides a Complete Picture of Job Requirements

Often a selection process focuses on a too-narrow aspect of job requirements, such as computing or accounting skills, without taking into account the other qualities needed for effective performance. A competency model provides a complete picture of what it takes to perform the work, thus ensuring that interviewers look for characteristics needed to do the job well in addition to required skills and knowledge. For example, successful performance may require an ability to work as part of a team, to balance multiple priorities, and to interact with people over whom the candidate has no direct

Exhibit 2.1 Benefits of Competency Models in HRM Systems

HRM System	Benefits
Selection	• Provides a complete picture of the job requirements • Increases the likelihood of hiring people who will succeed in the job • Minimizes the investment (both time and money) in people who may not meet the company's expectations • Ensures a more systematic interview process • Helps distinguish between competencies that are trainable and those that are more difficult to develop
Training and Development	• Enables people to focus on the skills, knowledge, and characteristics that have the most impact on effectiveness • Ensures that training and development opportunities are aligned with organizational values and strategies • Makes the most effective use of training and development time and dollars • Provides a framework for ongoing coaching and feedback
Appraisal	• Provides a shared understanding of what will be monitored and measured • Focuses and facilitates the performance appraisal discussion • Provides focus for gaining information about a person's behavior on the job
Succession Planning	• Clarifies the skills, knowledge, and characteristics required for the job or role in question • Provides a method to assess a candidate's readiness for the role • Focuses training and development plans to address missing competencies • Allows an organization to measure its "bench strength" (number of high-potential performers)

authority. Competency models also provide a method for interviewers to provide candidates with a clear and realistic picture of what will be expected of them.

Increases the Likelihood of Hiring People Who Will Succeed

Few things are worse than hiring a person for a key position who then fails to perform effectively. For many people who conduct interviews, the process feels like a guessing game. After speaking to a candidate for only a few hours (if that long), how can you determine if the person really has the potential to succeed in the job or is just someone who happens to write a persuasive résumé and make a good first impression?

Incorporating a validated competency model into selection systems addresses this problem by identifying the competencies with a strong correlation to high levels of performance on the job (Holdeman, Aldridge, and Jackson, 1996). This way, interviewers can weed out candidates who lack a critical set of skills, knowledge, or characteristics—or don't illustrate a potential to develop them—and focus instead on those with strong potential.

Minimizes Investment in People Who Do Not Meet Expectations

People who fail to perform the job they have been hired to do can have a tremendous impact on the productivity and profitability of an organization. Whether they leave due to poor performance, because they did not like the job, or because they did not fit in well with the organization's culture, the time and money spent in hiring and training them is wasted. In addition, it is expensive to put together a severance package and search for a new candidate, productivity suffers until the replacement is up to full performance capacity, and personnel changes can be disruptive for the affected team or work unit.

In her extensive work with Fortune 500 clients, Andrea Eisenberg, managing principal for Right Management Consultants' New York office and expert in the areas of retention and development, compares organizations that use competency models for selection and those that do not. "The optimal investment of human resources dollars happens when we allocate resources to developing those people who will be successful rather than allocating dollars to people without requisite competencies. Money spent to develop people with the right potential has a long-term payback and is key to retention. My clients who might have resisted the use of competencies initially have embraced their implementation when they see how a systematic approach to selection using this technique can enhance financial, personal, and organizational results" (personal communication, January, 1999). Using a validated competency model to select individuals who have a higher likelihood of meeting expectations can help minimize the time, dollars, and energy spent in selecting and training unsuccessful candidates.

Ensures a More Systematic Interview Process

Too often, selection decisions are based on the interviewer's initial impression of the job candidate. We feel a presence or absence of the "right chemistry" during the interview. Or we look at a person's list of accomplishments and are either impressed or concerned with how well his or her technical knowledge or experience fit with the job's requirements. Unfortunately, this is only part of the information needed to determine if a candidate will succeed, particularly for an entry-level position where a candidate may have the appropriate education but limited experience.

In an effective selection interview, the only variable is the candidate. Interviewers should be consistent in what they look for and how they determine if a candidate is right for the job. A competency model helps to make sure that all interviewers concentrate on the critical job-related factors required for success and are comparing apples to apples when discussing a candidate's qualifications. It can also facilitate agreement in hiring decisions by ensuring that everyone involved is working from the same criteria.

Helps Delineate Trainable Competencies

It is not uncommon to be generally impressed with a candidate. The person may possess a majority of the basic skills required and strike you as personable and articulate. Perhaps, though, you identify a few gaps in his or her abilities. Before making a hiring decision, you need to determine whether these gaps can be addressed through training and development. If the deficiency is lack of knowledge of a specific software application, you may decide to make an offer and enroll the person in a training program during his or her first week of orientation. If, however, the person indicates a general discomfort with computer technology, you have a different kind of decision to make. You must ask yourself if, given the strength of the candidate's other qualifications and the importance of computer literacy to the job, you wish to take a chance on the person's willingness and ability to learn the necessary technology. Similarly, if someone is personable and communicative but seems to have a low energy level, is the candidate a good match for a fast-paced customer service center?

A competency model can be very handy in answering these questions. Not only will it clarify the competencies most relevant to success, but it can pinpoint the attributes and capabilities that are more easily developed through training and those that are less trainable. Therefore, you can better assess the information you have about a job candidate, judge the quality and quantity of training the individual would need for effective performance, and then make an informed and realistic decision.

Benefits of Using a Competency-Based Training and Development System

Training and development systems have always sought to address the skills and knowledge required for successful job performance; however, they do not always target the competencies that are most relevant or have the greatest impact. Frequently, training and development efforts are driven by an immediate business need or problem (time management, working in a deregulated environment, negotiations) or sometimes by the latest fad or popular publication (total quality, empowerment, stress management, self-actualizing in the workplace). Using a competency model as the basis of a training and development system helps to avoid a short-term perspective or following fads and ensures that the system focuses on the right things rather than the latest things (Davis, 1996–1997). The four primary benefits of a competency-based training and development system are considered next.

Enables Focus on Relevant Behaviors and Skills

On the surface, clarifying a person's strengths and weaknesses as a leader, manager, team member, or technical specialist (sales, marketing, research and development, manufacturing, accounting, and the like) seems straightforward. Methods such as feedback from others, personal introspection, experience, some kind of testing, or a combination of these can provide an idea of what an individual does well and the areas that need improvement. But it is not always as easy as that.

How do you know, for example, when a strength is truly an advantage or a weakness is actually an area that needs further development? Someone might be people oriented and enjoy interacting with others, or a terrible negotiator, but if these are not relevant to job performance, to what extent should they be addressed? Clearly, being good at something is necessary but not sufficient; it must also be important to effective performance on the job. Competency models play an important part in keeping people and organizations focused on the skills, knowledge, and characteristics that affect job performance. These models can also help people better assess their current capabilities and determine the behaviors they need to develop to improve their effectiveness (Eubanks, Marshall, and O'Driscoll, 1990).

When people are clear about what it takes to succeed, they are better able to make decisions about training or development. They are less likely to sign up for programs that will not contribute to their job performance just to complete a certain required number of training hours. Finally, individuals are encouraged to become more proactive in their own development.

Ensures Alignment of Training and Development

A competency model provides focus for training and development opportunities and ensures that they are the ones essential to the success of the organization. In light of the hectic pace of many organizations and the importance of maintaining productivity, management must perceive training and development as relevant to business goals before they will support them. Systems that are reactionary or feature the most recent management and leadership fad are less likely to be viewed as credible and worthy of large expenditures of time and money. An effective training and development system must take a long-term view of organizational needs, and it must focus on developing the talent currently available in the workforce in order to meet these needs. A well-constructed competency model includes not only behaviors with a strong correlation to effectiveness on the job but also those required to support the organization's strategic direction and to develop and maintain the culture needed to achieve its business objectives. In this way, competency models can also help a human resource department determine whether additional training programs must be developed to address future organizational needs.

Makes the Most Effective Use of Training and Development

Focusing training programs and on-the-job development activities on the skills and behaviors that support the strategy and culture of an organization ensures that the time and money devoted to them will be well spent. Using a competency model helps remove the guesswork of where to focus scarce resources by differentiating between programs with the most impact on performance and those with little relevance to behaviors people need on the job.

Competency models can also help determine who needs which skills and at what point in their careers. Therefore people receive training and development when they have a use for it, increasing the likelihood that the relevant skills will be applied and reinforced through experiences on the job. This is better than the approach in which people work their way through every training program on the menu regardless of relevance to their current development needs or the requirements of their job.

Provides a Framework for Bosses and Coaches

An essential part of any training and development system is providing ongoing feedback, identifying the most useful on-the-job development opportunities, and reinforcing concepts and techniques learned in training programs—all part of the role of the boss or coach. The clarity and specificity of a competency model enable bosses and coaches to fulfill this role in a high-quality manner.

The model ensures that both the boss or coach and the direct report have a shared picture of what it takes to succeed in the job. In addition, it provides examples of behaviors that can be used as the basis for constructive development discussions. For example, a recommendation to increase self-sufficiency is more meaningful when a coach offers behaviors to support the competency (such as the ability to work independently for extended periods with minimal support or direction, or taking initiative). Furthermore, competency models can then be used as the starting point to help bosses or coaches and direct reports determine which on-the-job experiences will contribute to the development of these specific competencies.

Benefits of a Competency-Based Performance Appraisal System

Managers, human resource professionals, consultants, and academics have been trying to improve performance appraisal systems for almost three decades. Although an outside observer might say that progress has been made, many of the people involved on both sides of the process would say there is still plenty of room for improvement. Based on our experience and input from our clients, we have identified the following key issues:

- Lack of agreement on performance criteria
- Lack of balance in appraising what is accomplished and how it is accomplished
- Difficulty in collecting relevant and sufficient data
- Lack of opportunity for supervisors to observe behavior
- The inability to handle and process large amounts of data about an individual
- Lack of specificity and concreteness in discussions about performance deficiencies

We would not call the competency-based appraisal system a cure-all, but we do believe that the following benefits of incorporating competency models into the system can address many of the issues.

Provides a Shared Understanding of What Will Be Monitored and Measured

In this case, the introduction of a competency model into the appraisal system will specifically address two of the concerns on our list. Integrating the model into the appraisal forms ensures a balance between *what* gets done and *how* it gets done. The inclusion of a competency model signals that the organization is concerned not only with results but with the behaviors and manner with which those results are attained. As we've seen in other HRM systems, the competency model also provides the boss and his or her direct report with a shared picture of what is considered relevant and important to effective performance. The model, along with specific business objectives that have been developed with the direct report, specifically enumerates the performance criteria that will be used to measure effectiveness and success in that position. As a result, there is less room for subjectivity and misunderstandings among employees about what is expected of them during appraisal.

Focuses and Facilitates the Performance Appraisal Discussion

We've yet to meet a boss who looked forward to a performance appraisal discussion (though that could also be said for direct reports). The exception, of course, is when there is only good news, but that seems to be rare. Managers are faced with the challenge of discussing a person's behavior in a manner that is focused and useful and does not put the individual on the defensive. However, it is sometimes difficult to separate characteristics and attitudes from skills and knowledge to identify areas that need improvement. At other times, managers are overwhelmed by the vast universe of possible behaviors to discuss.

A competency-based appraisal system makes these types of issues less of a barrier. The skills, knowledge, and characteristics that are important to success are clearly described, and examples of behaviors are available to indicate when these competencies are being used effectively. A competency model provides a manager with a road map of where to begin the discussion and what areas to focus on. It may not make giving bad news any more pleasant, but at least it helps ensure that the discussion will be specific, concrete, and focused on behaviors.

Provides Focus for Gaining Information About Behavior

An ideal appraisal process includes a simple, accurate method for a boss to assess job performance. However, if the individual works in the field or the boss has direct reports in a variety of locations or is responsible for a large number of people, the process of assessing performance is unlikely to be simple or very accurate. And what about the boss who is new to a business unit or company? Where can she or he turn for reliable information about a direct report's performance?

By identifying the specific behaviors crucial for effective performance, competency models offer bosses a starting point. If, for example, the competency "teamwork" has been deemed critical, the boss can look for evidence of particular behaviors such as informing others about changes in priorities, assisting others in resolving conflicts, and so on.

Some companies have begun to use the 360-degree feedback process to facilitate the collection of this data. As you will recall, this process involves gathering observations about performance from a wide range of people: colleagues, the individual's direct reports, customers, suppliers, and so on. In this case, a boss can base appraisal feedback on not only his or her own perception, but also the perceptions of people who are perhaps better positioned to make an assessment.

Although there are some issues regarding the use of a 360-degree feedback process when making decisions regarding salary and promotion, many organizations have found the result—an accurate and comprehensive picture of an individual's performance—a compelling reason to consider this option. Mark Edwards, founder and CEO of TEAMS International, a Right Management Consultant company, says, "Competency models are a powerful tool that communicates very clearly to employees what is expected of them and how to be successful. [One client's employee] (a huge public utility), after reviewing his feedback for the first time, said, 'I finally understand what this organization is all about.' This feedback is truly a gift that recognizes, develops, and motivates people to succeed" (personal communication, Jan. 18, 1999).

Benefits of Using a Competency-Based Succession Planning System

Many organizations profess a preference for promoting from within. This approach makes sense on numerous levels: candidates are already familiar with the business's functions, culture, and strategic objectives; retention maximizes the value of selection and development expenditures; and advancement opportunities serve to motivate a workforce. Following this dictate, however, is not simple. Effective succession planning systems comprise four key components:

- A list of the positions under consideration
- Agreement among the decision makers about what is required for success in each position
- A list of who's ready now and why
- A list of who will be ready soon, accompanied by the person's development needs and recommended actions to close the gaps

It could be said that succession planning borrows elements from other HRM systems: selection (criteria for successful performance and identification of those people most likely to succeed), training and development (clarification of strengths and weaknesses, development planning, skill training, and on-the-job experience), and appraisal systems (monitoring progress, coaching, and evaluation). Taken together, these processes help organizations identify and develop the individuals they believe have the potential to fill specific and often more senior jobs. It follows, then, that if competency models can add value to these other systems, they will also contribute to the effectiveness of the succession planning system. Following are specific benefits.

Clarifies Required Skills, Knowledge, and Characteristics

Before an organization can begin to consider filling a key position, it must identify the requirements of the job and the factors that will contribute to successful performance. The development and validation of a competency model helps to define the abilities necessary to fill the role and also those behaviors that are strong predictors of success. Often, the process also reveals significant differences in the factors that contribute to effective performance in various jobs. For example, the requirements for the successful performance of plant managers or regional leaders may vary depending on location, market size, scope of the business, and so on. The investment of time and money to develop an individual for a key position and the importance of the position to the business's success make these succession planning decisions particularly critical. Of course, a competency-based succession planning system cannot guarantee that the right decision will be made. It can, however, identify the skills, knowledge, and characteristics needed in the position and the behaviors that led to successful performance in the past.

Provides a Method to Assess Candidate Readiness

Determining if and when candidates are ready for a role requires a method to assess their strengths and weaknesses. A competency model coupled with a 360-degree feedback process works well in addressing this need. The competency model serves to create an agreed-upon list of the criteria required by the job. As a result, discussions among decision makers about a candidate's readiness are focused on the relevant attributes and characteristics. The use of 360-degree feedback can further improve these discussions by providing perspective from those who are directly affected by the candidate's day-to-day behavior.

Focuses Training and Development Plans to Address Missing Competencies

Effective succession plans not only identify individuals who are ready for promotion but also create a road map for developing other high-potential candidates. Again, competency models and the 360-degree feedback process create a powerful pairing to pinpoint the areas that require improvement before a candidate can advance in an organization. The model describes the competencies needed in the role, and the feedback provides a method of assessing a candidate's current competencies. With this information, an individual—working alone or with a coach—can determine the classroom and on-the-job training required to close skill and knowledge gaps. Candidates can also prepare themselves by seeking out the types of experiences they are likely to encounter in the particular role in the future.

Allows an Organization to Measure Its Bench Strength

Good coaches know the strengths and weaknesses of the players on their bench, and they don't get caught short when it comes time to make a substitution. Organizations would do well to follow suit. The point at which one is trying to fill a key position is an unfortunate time to discover a shortage of high-potential employees. A competency-based succession planning system allows a company to assess its bench strength. Individual and aggregate assessments of competency levels and relevant behaviors can help identify the presence or absence of key capabilities at an organizational level. This information can then be used to make decisions related to other human resource management systems. For example, the organization can determine if its selection and training systems are successful in attracting and developing people with the right mix of skills, knowledge, and characteristics required to ensure the business's success over the long term.

How Are Organizations Using Competency Models?

No matter what business issue a company is facing—a culture change due to a merger or an acquisition, shifts in business strategy and values, or the need to respond to tactical moves of the competition—the solution begins and ends with its people. It is the company's workforce that must adapt to any change, align behavior with new business priorities, or be readied to meet the challenges of tomorrow (Horney and Koonce, 1995). As you will see in the following case studies, competency models offer a method to identify the abilities people must possess to address these business issues and ensure that human resource systems focus on the behaviors that are critical to the organization's success.

Using Strategy to Determine Training Needs: The Geon Corporation

Geon, formerly an operating division of the B. F. Goodrich Company, is now (after a leveraged buyout) an independent manufacturer of polyvinyl chloride (PVC) resins and compounds and has been undergoing a dynamic transformation since going out on its own. Having converted to a more horizontal management structure in which more people are decision makers and creators of strategy, the organization's success increasingly depends on maximizing every employee's performance and on ensuring quick and effective responses to changing customer and market needs.

Because senior management recognized the primary importance of developing people at all levels of the organization, Carol Schmidt, formerly director of customer operations, was put in charge of an initiative to ensure that development and learning were an integral part of the culture. As head of organizational learning, her task was to make learning part of every job so that people would be continually preparing themselves to meet the next challenge.

The timing was right for one of Geon's businesses: the compound business, which had just clarified its vision for the year 2000 and wanted to identify the skills people would need to get there. Having decided that competency models would be a useful tool to help enhance development and learning, Schmidt engaged a team of consultants experienced at developing such models, and the process began.

The consultants conducted interviews with twenty-five people from the senior business team and other levels. They asked the following questions:

- What specific demands do the year 2000 goals place on you and your area?
- What obstacles might prevent you from achieving those goals and what factors can enhance your ability to achieve them?

- What leadership behaviors or skills currently being used in Geon must be maintained for the company to be successful? Why?

- What leadership behaviors or skills need to be changed or are currently weak within Geon? Why? How can they be enhanced?

- What do you personally see as strengths you want to leverage or areas you will need to develop in achieving the year 2000 goals?

When the interviewers asked what kind of behaviors people in the compound business had to exhibit to achieve the business's objectives, the answers they received were fairly consistent. From this list of behaviors it was easy to identify critical skills. For example, everyone agreed that there was a need for more problem-solving and analytical skills, and for more effective conflict resolution skills.

After the initial interviews, Schmidt and the consultants developed a draft model and performed a validation study where they asked all the interviewees to rate each identified competency in terms of how essential it was to effective job performance. Thus the organization could confirm that it had identified competencies that were perceived as relevant and important. Once the model was finalized, they turned it over to functional leaders within the compound business for use in discussions with their staff and the prioritization of training and development needs.

As a result of the interviewing process, Schmidt also uncovered a need for employees at all levels to improve their use of information technology. In fact, this area was ranked as the most important by a majority of the respondents; Schmidt herself says that she sees the need for technology training as the "number one reason I was given this job. Our competitive advantage in the future will be dependent on technology. We have to develop a more formal structure to develop people's skills in this area, especially now that we've got networked enterprise software, which everybody is going to have to understand and use. Even at the basic level of using personal computers, there are skill gaps that need to be addressed. So we are also developing a competency model for

PC users, with a goal of having every PC user certified to a basic level by the year 2000."

The compound business is now beginning to use the competency model in the performance planning process as well as for training purposes to identify and address crucial skill gaps among its employees. The general manager of the business is using it in appraisals of his direct reports and encouraging them to do likewise with their people. The model is also expected to help with the selection process for recruiting people from outside and moving internal people into new roles. It has also helped people to clarify a culture change issue. As Schmidt says, "Three years ago, if someone at Geon had looked at that model, he would have said it was a competency model for managers only. Now we expect everyone in the organization to have ownership of the job, to take initiative, to help develop others; in that sense, everyone plays a management role now."

Schmidt's main advice to others about to embark on a similar project is to make sure that senior management is solidly behind it. "The other thing that's really important is to be able to educate people on the value of the project by showing them how it ties together all sorts of HR initiatives, and how they in turn relate to competitive advantage. At times that can be tricky, because training benefits are hard to measure, so it's not always possible to show them hard-and-fast numbers. What you need to do is to make a convincing case that these things will improve general excellence and help to ensure reliable service and product quality."

Schmidt has found that telling people at Geon about other organizations' use of competency models helps her make her case. "When our managers find out that our competitors and customers are putting time and effort into this kind of project, they are more willing to consider the process as a necessary one."

Schmidt's next project is to start working with the general managers' team to develop a competency model for managers. Based on the model they produce, the company can then begin to design training programs for managers. She is also developing a functional competency model, building on the original model, based on department managers' perceptions of what functional skills they need their people to have. She expects that eventually Geon will have a model for each functional position—plant managers, administrative assistants, and others—and hopes that someday the company will have one for each specific job.

Aligning Human Resource Management Systems: Brooklyn Union Gas

At Brooklyn Union, a utility company providing natural gas to New York private residences, businesses, and government institutions in Brooklyn, Staten Island, and parts of Queens, competency models first evolved as a means to identify and develop people with high potential to become managers. As Marc Baca, former management process consultant at Brooklyn Union, puts it, "We wanted to assess high-potential individuals with a set of measurement tools that were specific to our industry and our organization. We were not looking for an off-the-shelf tool. The dilemma we faced was that we did not have the criteria to assess them against. We had no benchmark for either evaluation or feedback." Senior management decided to bring in an outside consultant to assist with the development of a set of competencies against which area managers could be measured, and to incorporate the model into an assessment tool to determine an individual's potential for success in the job. Says Baca, "Based on those competencies, senior management could begin to get feedback on our high-potential people and develop them to be successful area managers in the future."

Once this process was in place, the idea began to percolate that it would be useful to develop competency models for all levels of management. Human Resources decided to modify the initial set of competencies (which had pertained specifically to area managers) to reduce their number and make the model more generic and manageable. They used interviews, focus groups, and surveys to come up with a set of ten core competencies that were important for every management employee in the company.

When the competency model was first developed, interviews were held with officers and area heads to get a clear picture from them of what they expected the organization to look like five and ten years into the future. During this phase, Human Resources also met with people from the strategic planning area and high-performing managers to get their views on the same issue.

In the second phase of competency model development, a large number of managerial jobs were selected at random; job descriptions were studied and job analyses were performed. Focus groups with people throughout the organization led to a draft of a general competency model for managers, which was then validated through further focus groups and interviews. Based on what had been learned in the second round of groups and interviews, the model was modified to reflect reality as closely as possible.

In the last phase, each competency that had been identified was broken down into two or three observable behaviors. For example, the competency "creating value for the customer" broke down into the items "ask questions," "listen actively" and "use customer feedback to ensure that needs are being met." The focus was very much on behaviors that are value driven and concrete, so that the competency model would help managers both to perform their day-to-day jobs and to attain goals that are aligned with the company's strategic direction.

Because the first model was developed with a small group of people in mind, proactive communication about the project was limited. Although there was senior-level support for the project, there was a feeling that the model was not widely applicable, and as a result the competencies were not used as originally intended. The second time around, because the project involved many more management employees through the use of interviews, focus groups, and surveys, communication was a top priority. This effort, coupled with highly visible senior-level support (the project's chief champions were the company's president and its SVP of Human Resources), ensured that the competency model would be put to use.

Now competency models form an integral part of Brooklyn Union's selection and performance management systems. The competencies have been incorporated into hiring criteria, so management trainees are expected to possess the ten core competencies. Baca says, "Too often candidates are hired for their skills, and no attention is given to cultural affinity. Many of those employees end up leaving, which is costly to the company and detrimental to the employee. Our approach, I believe, helps us find people who are not only qualified but also will feel comfortable working in our culture." In the appraisal process, the use of competency models has helped managers focus on both the what (the accomplishment of preestablished goals) and the how (the manner in which those goals are attained).

"Before," says Baca, "the performance appraisal was based on the values of the company. As it turns out, managers feel much more comfortable evaluating their subordinates in terms of competencies rather than values. Because the competencies are so behavior oriented, the appraisal process feels less subjective. When employees realized that, it was a big step forward in acceptance of the model."

Baca also feels that the model has helped change Brooklyn Union's culture, particularly in the sense of enabling people to become more strategically aligned. "In the past, the culture of this company, like that of most utilities, was inwardly focused. There was little emphasis on things like communication or development, whether of the self or others. Now, people are grasping that not only do we expect them to be good communicators, and to be responsible for their own and others' development, they are going to be judged on those competencies."

Asked what advice he might give to other people about to embark on this process, Baca says, "Make sure you have a reason to do it. Don't develop a competency model just because every other company is building one. And make sure you understand what is meant by competencies. As I see it, they are the set of skills, knowledge, and personal attributes or values, all working together, that someone brings to the job. It will take some time to identify those competencies which can be truly meaningful to people."

Enhancing Training and Development and Selection Systems: Continental Grain Company

Continental Grain is a privately owned company that has produced animal protein (poultry, cattle, pork, and chicken) and traded grain, propane, and other commodities for more than seventy-five years; it recently diversified into financial services. In its case, developing a competency model was part of an effort to ensure that the company continued to succeed for the next seventy-five years. Continental Grain had been going through significant change as it attempted to define what businesses to be in and what values were needed to take it into the next century. Paul Fribourg, the CEO, had a vision of a boundaryless organization in which each division nurtured and grew new, value-added businesses while freely sharing learning and information across organizational lines to help other divisions succeed. Fribourg also had a picture of what the leader of the future at Continental Grain would need to look like in order to achieve this vision. Dwight Coffin, VP of Human Resources, was charged with translating this vision of the future leader into a set of clear and measurable competencies that could be used for training and development and, eventually, appraisal.

At the corporate level, the focus was on developing a model of managerial competencies designed to communicate to senior-level managers around the world what would be expected of them and to help them identify development goals. A consultant was brought in to help define the senior manager competencies, develop a list of behavior examples for each one, and convert the competency model into a 360-degree feedback questionnaire. (The questionnaire is used as part of the company's strategic leadership program, which is required for all middle and senior managers. During the program, managers receive feedback on their use of the critical competencies as perceived by their direct reports, colleagues, and boss. Half a day is devoted to the analysis and interpretation of the feedback, and the rest of the four-day workshop uses a large-scale business simulation and skill development exercises to provide managers with training opportunities related to the competencies they want to develop further.)

Competency models were also being developed at the business level. In the poultry division, for example, another competency project focused on enhancing selection and recruitment systems in order to reduce the turnover of hourly employees. The division began the project by undertaking a thorough interviewing process for hourly employees and then went on to build competency models for each job. The program has measurably reduced turnover by providing guidelines on what to ask prospective employees to determine if they have the competencies required to stick with the job. "Essentially," says Dwight Coffin, "if you're interviewing someone about deboning chickens, you need to make sure they have the ability to do repetitive work and enjoy it. That's the way to cut down on turnover. So we have come up with a number of questions designed to elicit that information. That way, the people doing the interviewing can quickly spot recruits with the potential to stay with the job."

When asked what advice he might give to other organizations interested in developing competency models to help them meet their business goals, Coffin said, "First of all, have some patience. And, secondly, try to view the organization in a boundaryless manner; don't look at the different divisions as though they were different species of animals. Third, spend whatever time is necessary to get the support of senior management, rather than just HR support. We got out of the HR mode and are in the business mode; we dropped the jargon and presented it to them in their own terms. In fact, we never even used the term 'competency model.' Instead, we talked about helping them to identify people to hire and helping them to decide which people to promote. I think the fact that we didn't couch it in HR language made all the difference."

Achieving Business Strategy: Household International

When Bill Aldinger took over as the CEO of Household International, a major financial services company, in 1994, his message to employees was that he wanted them and the company to be "the best in their class." What was needed to translate his vision into reality was a clear definition of what that "best" looked like—what managers at Household needed to know and do to succeed for themselves and the organization.

So Aldinger charged the Human Resources Training Department with the task of determining which competencies were crucial in a corporate culture that was changing dramatically: rather than leaving decision-making processes up to a few senior executives, the new emphasis was on creating "leaders at all levels." The HR people then went out and talked to the senior team and managers throughout the organization, asking them to name the qualities and skills they felt were most important to achieving Aldinger's goal. They wound up with what Sue Keenan, AVP of Human Resources, called a "huge laundry list of competencies," which they analyzed to find the common themes.

Having arrived at a list of about twenty management competencies, it was time to start looking for a feedback instrument they could use to evaluate managers on their use of those competencies. They purchased one from an outside firm and had it customized to include such competencies as risk taking, customer focus, coaching, sponsoring change, and encouraging continuous improvement, all of which were considered vital to Household's achieving its strategic goals.

The model became the basis of the curriculum for the Leaders at All Levels program, which focused on the key competencies that had been defined. Once the feedback program was under way, the next step was to integrate the competency model into the organization's performance management system to ensure that managers' on-the-job behavior would align with the values and expectations that had been articulated.

As the various applications of the model were implemented, a need for fine-tuning became apparent, as there had not really been much distinction made between the behaviors expected of senior managers and those required of other managers.

Says Jeanne Gruner, VP of training and development, "Based on the feedback we got from the organization's senior people, we realized that certain competencies were more geared to managing than leading, or at least the behaviors we had identified as demonstrating those competencies were more managerial. For example, when we talk about a manager inspiring people, we may be talking about a one-on-one interaction. In the case of a leader, we are talking about leading a large team, or moving a large group to where they need to be. That involves describing the vision in a broader context. So we kept inspiring as a managerial competency, while the competency for senior managers is now called inspirational leadership."

In addition to developing a competency model for senior-level people, Gruner plans to come up with a competency model for salaried workers at the associate or nonexempt level. "The present model needs a little tweaking at both the high and low ends before it can be really useful to the entire population at Household. The current one has been most successful with middle managers. But it has also helped the organization as a whole to figure out what we need to do in order to get where we want to go."

Keenan offers this advice to other companies embarking on a competency model project: "The support of senior management throughout the project will help to keep it visible and also encourage everyone's ongoing commitment through what can be a long process."

Supporting Large-Scale Organizational Change: National Bank

After National Bank merged with another large banking institution, many people in the finance organization of the new National found themselves dealing with a whole different chain of command and a new set of priorities. At the same time, the Finance organization was in the process of examining all the methods and approaches used by both banks and determining which alternative the new merged entity should adopt—or whether it should seek to find a third way that would be better than the other two. As Ellen Nichols, a VP of Human Resources, expresses it, "Every decision made meant a new process for at least half the group. So first they found themselves working with people they weren't familiar with, then they were expected to change their priorities, and then even the technical processes they were used to, like general ledger processes, changed on them."

Furthermore, after the merger—the second for National in two years—there was a tremendous emphasis on teamwork, diversity, and issues such as internal customer focus, which had never gotten much attention under the previous regime. So rather than being evaluated on their technical accomplishments alone, accountants and others in the group were suddenly being judged in terms of their sensitivity to issues no one had ever mentioned to them before.

There was also the issue of dealing with a changing external environment, one much more competitive than any that had been previously confronted. "With everything changing so drastically both inside and outside the organization," says Nichols, "it was no longer possible for anyone to operate on autopilot."

Faced with the need to create a new integrated vision and identity for the function, communicate the new values to its people, and help them understand what was required and expected of them day to day, the Finance organization decided that competency models were the way to go. It was determined that the first development effort would focus on models for the director level and above, with a model for the vice-president level and below to follow.

Finance wanted a functional model that would clarify what the critical factors were for success in the newly merged organization. Such a model would focus neither on leadership behaviors per se nor on knowledge of accounting rules; instead, it would articulate what skills and behaviors were required and how people could expect to be judged in a best-in-its-class finance organization. A consulting firm was called in, and its people began interviewing the senior team and managers in the function, holding focus groups, and distributing a questionnaire that asked people which skills they saw as important to effectiveness in directors' functional roles. Based on the answers to the first method of data gathering, a second questionnaire was developed in order to validate the hypotheses about crucial skills. Finally, the CFO of the organization and a team of senior managers helped the consultants come up with a final draft of the model for the director level and above.

The next stage involved incorporating the model into the performance appraisal process. It was decided that every year when a director listed his or her business objectives, he or she would also have to name the competencies required to achieve those objectives and outline a plan for strengthening those competencies if necessary.

In looking back on the success of the development phase, Nichols cites the internal need that drove it as key to its effectiveness: "Our people were hungry for some kind of structure. After going through two mergers, they knew they needed help, and they wanted it badly. And then we involved as many line people as possible in developing the model, which made for tremendous buy-in."

Implementation, too, has proved to be highly successful. Again Nichols attributes this to what she calls the "hunger for structure. People wanted a performance management system that really helped them to focus on the skills they needed to do their jobs well; they wanted to understand what would make the difference between mediocrity and real success. In the past, the challenge might have been to train managers in how to use the new performance management process. Now, it's helping them keep up with all the staff who have a hunger for it. People want to use the competency model because it can help them in their own jobs, their own development."

Concluding Remarks

Although the competency model projects just described were undertaken for very different purposes, certain common themes emerge in the advice given by the managers involved. Translated into specific guidelines, their recommendations might be expressed as follows:

- Always make sure the competency model project addresses a specific business need, and that people in the organization understand the strategic reasons for undertaking it.
- Senior management support is a must to generate commitment at all levels of the company and to ensure that the competency model initiative will accomplish the purposes for which it is intended.
- Communicate clearly and frequently about the project's purpose and the progress being made throughout the duration of the process.
- Involve as many people as possible in planning and implementing the development of the model and the human resources initiative it supports. Early involvement is the best way to prevent resistance and suspicion from taking root.
- Ensure that the behaviors on the competency model are relevant to people's jobs and that people perceive that relevance.
- Be willing to devote the necessary time and energy to formally plan for the development and implementation of the model, allocating appropriate resources and monitoring progress to ensure you stay on course in meeting your objectives.

Keeping these guidelines in mind as you embark on your own competency modeling project should go a long way toward ensuring its success.

Chapter Three

Competency Models

Laying the Groundwork

As any builder will tell you, laying a good foundation is the first step for constructing something of enduring value. Competency models are no exception. In this chapter, we discuss the four areas you need to consider to ensure a solid foundation for a competency model project.

1. *Determine the objectives and scope of the project.* Why are we doing it? What jobs, functions, or business units will we target? What method will we use to develop the model? Who will carry out the work?

2. *Clarify implementation goals and standards.* What is the intended result of the project? How will we know when we've achieved it?

3. *Create an action plan.* What tasks are involved? Who is responsible for carrying them out? When must they be completed? What resources are required?

4. *Identify individuals who meet, exceed, or fall below established performance criteria.* What does successful performance on the job look like? What job outputs or results will be examined? Against whose performance will we test our findings? (Boyatzis reviewed these questions in his 1982 work, *The Competent Manager.*)

Before addressing these issues, let's look briefly at the reasons careful planning is so important.

Benefits of Planning

Building a competency model requires complex activities such as scheduling dozens of one-on-one interviews and focus group meetings, coordinating the project team's calendars to arrange data analysis and review meetings, and timing production of the draft documents for review by key stakeholders before proceeding to the next step. Coordinating a project of this magnitude and ensuring that it is completed on time and on budget is much more manageable with a detailed action plan to help guide the work and monitor progress toward project goals. In our experience, a competency model project loses credibility and the support of even its staunchest proponents when it is carried out poorly or perceived as being managed in a sloppy, unprofessional manner. A solid, well-organized implementation plan, conversely, sends a signal that the project is being managed well; it helps build support and ensures attention and the commitment of resources. A good implementation plan also minimizes the impact of unexpected problems or circumstances on the project's time and budget constraints.

The benefits of planning are realized at three levels: individual, project team, and organization.

- For individuals, it allows them to integrate this project with other activities.

- At the project team level, planning facilitates mutual agreement of purpose among team members at the start of the project; it ensures that team members understand their responsibilities and those of other team members; and it encourages ongoing lateral communication during the project's duration.

- At the organizational level, planning assigns and coordinates responsibilities across groups; it becomes the basis for recognizing and resolving group conflicts; and it helps with the allocation of resources and the identification of shortfalls.

The project sponsor or manager must also decide when and how to involve people whose support is critical to the project's success and widespread use. But first you need to familiarize yourself with the steps involved in developing a competency model. Identifying key stakeholders and gaining their commitment will be discussed in a later chapter.

Step One: Determine Objectives and Scope

To lay the groundwork, first determine the objectives and scope of the project. There are four steps in this process:

1. Identify the business need or needs that the competency model will address.
2. Identify the jobs, functions, or business units that the model will target.
3. Determine the method for developing the competency model.
4. Determine the makeup of the project team.

Let's take a closer look at each of these steps.

Identify the Business Need

A clearly defined business need will help ensure ongoing support for the project and that the efforts of all participants remain focused on a clear objective. As we've seen, competency models can add value to the selection, training and development, performance appraisal, and succession planning processes; however, any such HRM system enhancement should be made with a specific business need in mind. For example, a business need of maximizing productivity can drive a desire to improve the selection and training and development systems to ensure that people are hired who demonstrate the skills, behaviors, and traits needed for high productivity (high energy, team orientation, analytic skills, high work standards, and the like) and that training encourages further development of those behaviors. Other business needs we have seen organizations address through the development of competency models include the following:

- Attracting top talent
- Retaining key employees
- Ensuring that skills are available for the future business environment
- Aligning cross-organizational teams to get products to market faster
- Aligning people's behavior with organizational values and strategy

The process of defining this business need will benefit from as much input from all levels of management as possible. Strategic leaders can provide insight about the business's priorities and future direction. Line managers can offer feedback regarding skill and knowledge gaps among their direct reports and identify opportunities to enhance business processes. Including these individuals at the development stage will also begin the critical process of building commitment to and fostering enthusiasm for the project.

Identify the Target Population

Once you have a defined business need, you can consider the jobs, functions, or business units that require enhancement to meet that need. If a business area is undergoing a change in strategy or is facing a need to maintain a competitive edge, you may wish to develop a set of competencies that apply to the particular work unit or cross-organizational team. If you wish to increase the productivity of people in a particular job, such as sales associate, you will want to develop a competency model to enhance the selection, training and development, and performance management of individuals in that role. If your business need is global in nature—instilling a specific company value such as customer focus throughout the work-force, for example—you may wish to identify the core competencies every associate must demonstrate regardless of level or position to reflect this value. Keep in mind, however, that a competency model is most meaningful when it provides behavioral examples of the identified competencies. Therefore, the end result of the project should include the behaviors demonstrating effective customer service, for example, for all roles that require this competency.

Determine Method of Approach

Two general approaches for developing competency models are outlined in Exhibit 3.1. (See also Mansfield, 1996, for review of the implications of these approaches.)

Starting from Scratch. This method calls for developing a competency model using data collected internally, from interviews with incumbents and informed observers, focus groups, and on-the-job observations. The data are also analyzed internally to identify the competencies seen as significant to effective performance. Starting from scratch is appropriate for developing a competency model for any job, function, or role in the organization. It is time-consuming but yields results that are role- and company-specific.

Starting with a Validated Competency Model. The second approach to developing a competency model parallels the first. The primary difference is the use of a validated model as the starting point instead of extensive interviews and observations of incumbents on the job. This may save time on data collection, analysis, and validation, but generic models may not address specific jobs or positions and may not highlight the technical skills and knowledge required for success. This method is best suited for leadership and management roles that cut across several functions and for positions that require limited technical skills and knowledge. Chapter Five discusses this approach in more detail.

Exhibit 3.1 Two Approaches to Developing Competency Models

Starting from Scratch	*Starting with a Validated Model*
1. Identify performance criteria for individuals and work units.	1. Identify performance criteria for individuals and work units.
2. Identify individuals and work units that meet, exceed, and fall below the performance criteria.	2. Identify individuals and work units that meet, exceed, and fall below the performance criteria.
3. Interview job incumbents and informed observers.	
4. Observe job incumbents directly—"a day in the life."	
5. Develop interim competency model—analyze data for themes and patterns and look for differences between exceptional and standard performers.	
6. Administer a survey and/or conduct focus groups to include a wider population and test the degree of relevance and importance of the competencies to the job.	3. Administer a survey and/or conduct focus groups to include a wider population and test the degree of relevance and importance of given competencies to the job.
7. Analyze survey or focus group data and refine the model.	4. Analyze the survey or focus group data and refine the model.
8. Validate the model: administer a 360-degree questionnaire to identify competencies that correlate with exceptional performers.	5. Validate the model: administer a 360-degree questionnaire to identify competencies that correlate with exceptional performers.
9. Finalize the model.	6. Finalize the model.

Determine the Makeup of the Project Team

The size and makeup of the project team should depend on the scope of your project. A project team of five to nine people (depending on the scope of the study) serves the needs of most projects. The makeup of your team should include the following people: individuals who will be responsible for implementing and using the competency model, key stakeholders who will be affected by the project, and a visible sponsor who can act as its advocate within the organization.

Although people can learn many of the techniques involved in developing a high-quality competency model, we recommend seeking for your team one or two individuals with experience and practice in competency model development to help ensure the development of a high-quality final product. Those trained in observation techniques and experienced in interpreting behavior will also be helpful, as will others who have special understanding of the target job and the time management and organizational skills needed to facilitate the project's progress.

Step Two: Clarify Implementation Goals and Standards

Create an Implementation Goal Statement

Clarifying the implementation goal early in the process will provide direction for the project, serve as the basis for determining individual action steps, and help you determine when the project is complete. The goal should be a specific objective expressed in terms of performance or output. A good implementation goal will be all of the following:

- Specific
- Challenging, yet realistic and attainable
- Consistent with available resources
- Consistent with the organization's policies and operating procedures
- Measurable
- Inclusive of an expected completion date

An example of a goal statement for a competency modeling project is, "To develop a competency model for senior-level executives that can be used for training and development in each line of business by the end of the second quarter."

Establish Implementation Standards

Implementation standards address quality, quantity, and timing that must be met to achieve your goal. The standards developed will create an "excellence model" that describes how the work will be done and evaluated. This set of standards is also used to identify what actions must be taken to meet them. Examples of standards for the implementation goal stated in the previous paragraph could include those shown in Exhibit 3.2.

Step Three: Develop an Action Plan

An action plan is the primary tool to manage the workload, review and appraise project progress, and communicate with project team members and key stakeholders about the work to be done. This tool

Exhibit 3.2 Implementation Goal and Standards Worksheet

Implementation Goal:

To develop a competency model for senior-level executives that can be used for training and development in each line of business by the end of the second quarter.

Standards

1. Data collection does not disrupt day-to-day activities.
2. Key stakeholders from each line of business and function perceive the competencies to be relevant and important to the on-the-job success of senior executives in their areas.
3. The competency model is aligned and consistent with current leadership development activities.
4. The project does not exceed budget.
5. The project is completed with a minimum of external resources.
6. Senior managers are actively involved in developing and finalizing the model.
7. The model can readily be converted into a 360-degree questionnaire.
8. The model balances length (manageable number of competencies and behavior examples) with completeness (fully describes the requirements for success).

will also aid in determining the resource requirements (people, time, money, and technological tools) for the project's completion, information that will be useful when approaching decision makers and stakeholders for their support. These requirements will vary depending on the scope of your project, whether you conduct the study internally or employ the help of consultants experienced in competency model development, and the number of people you include on your team. We have seen studies take anywhere from six weeks to two years to complete. As a general rule of thumb, most studies can be conducted within two to three months.

Another integral part of the planning stage is the identification of possible problems and the development of preventive and contingent actions to address them. The more foresight given to the planning process, the more likely your chances for successfully implementing your project.

List the Project Action Steps

At a minimum, an action plan should include the following:

- *Action steps:* Break down the work to be done and the deliverables into tasks and activities.
- *Accountabilities:* Identify individuals and groups responsible for carrying out each action step.
- *Schedule:* Set start and completion dates for specific actions, milestones, and the whole project.
- *Resource requirements:* Identify the equipment, people, money, or other resources needed to complete the action steps.

See Exhibit 3.3 for a sample action plan.

As the first step in creating an action plan, perform a quick brainstorm of the work to be done to accomplish your goal and meet your standards. Next, arrange the steps in chronological order, adding steps as gaps become apparent, and assign the person who will be responsible for each action. Finally, review the actions against

Exhibit 3.3 Action Planning Worksheet

Action Steps	Resource Requirements	Accountability	Start Date	Finish Date
1. Determine list of interviewees and focus group participants	Access to database, access to incumbents	Client	1/1	1/3
2. Prepare topics for the focus group ("A" group)		Manus	1/1	1/3
3. Write invitation letter to focus group		Manus	1/2	1/3
4. Write interview questions		Manus	1/2	1/3
5. Schedule focus groups	Administrative support	Client/ Manus	1/4	1/8
6. Schedule face-to-face and tele-phone interviews	Administrative support	Client	1/4	1/8
7. Send invitation letter to focus group	Access to database	Client	1/5	1/9
8. Distribute inter-view questions to interviewees	Internal mail	Client	1/5	1/9
9. Conduct focus groups	Private conference rooms, flip charts	Manus	1/20	2/5
10. Conduct interviews	Private conference rooms	Manus	1/20	2/10
11. Develop initial hypothesis model		Manus	2/12	2/14
12. Review status of Competency Model	Meeting room, senior management team	Manus	2/17	
13. Develop survey	Software, if needed	Manus	2/18	2/20
14. Distribute survey	Internal mail	Client	2/22	2/24

Exhibit 3.3   Action Planning Worksheet, cont'd.

Action Steps	Resource Requirements	Accountability	Start Date	Finish Date
15. Draft competency model		Manus	3/15	3/18
16. Validate competency model with research participants		Manus	3/20	3/27
17. Finalize and present report to company		Manus	4/5	
18. Validate competency model with nonparticipating groups	Access to nonparticipants	Manus	4/7	4/20

your standards. If, for example, the inclusion of all lines of business is a standard, do the action steps ensure that this standard will be achieved?

Identify Potential Problems and Their Likely Causes

Any number of events, conditions, and situations could potentially derail the plan. Some circumstances are predictable—others are not. Advanced planning for the likely obstacles will lessen their impact should they occur and also help to minimize the impact of any unforeseen events that arise.

Once you have defined your goal and standards and determined what steps need to be taken to attain them, ask yourself what problems are most likely to occur during implementation. The six most common problem areas are these:

1. Time (other obligations, changing priorities)
2. Control (influence of key stakeholders, competing goals and expectations of different individuals)

3. Power and politics (influence of the formal and informal organization, organizational policy and procedures, interested parties)

4. Resources (availability of people and dollars)

5. Resistance (stemming from conflicting goals, comfort with the status quo)

6. Skill (people's ability to perform the tasks required in a high-quality manner)

To conduct your potential problem analysis, review each action step and the plan as a whole, and ask, "What could go wrong here?" As the list of potential problems could be quite long, it will benefit from some focus. Therefore, assess each potential problem in terms of its probability and impact (should it occur). Make it your first priority to develop preventive and contingent actions for the potential problems with the highest probability and impact. If time permits, you may then wish to develop actions for those that are less critical.

Develop Preventive and Contingent Actions

Before determining the appropriate actions to address these obstacles, you must first identify the likely causes of each of your high-priority potential problems. With this information, you can better direct preventive action toward eliminating or limiting the likely cause. You may find that modifying the original plan—adding or changing action steps, reassessing accountabilities, or changing completion dates—will lessen the likelihood of a problem occurring.

As a final step in the planning process, develop contingency actions to address any problems that occur despite your efforts to prevent them. This step will help you to quickly and efficiently resolve these circumstances rather than merely react to them haphazardly.

Exhibit 3.4 is a job aid that may be useful to help you do the following:

- Itemize the potential problems most likely to arise in implementing the plan.
- Determine how likely each is (probability) and how serious each would be (impact).
- Develop a list of preventive actions that would minimize the chance of each problem occurring.
- Assign accountability for the preventive actions.
- Develop a list of contingent actions (that is, what will you do if the problem occurs anyway?).
- Assign accountability for the contingent actions.

Once you have modified your original implementation plan to take into account potential problems and preventive measures (as well as the preparation of contingency actions should they be necessary), you have a game plan for implementation. This reality-based document should equip you to deal with almost every eventuality that might arise. It will also serve to provide people outside the project team with step-by-step information about the development process.

Establish Communication Channels

Ongoing communication about the progress of the project is vital to its success. The project sponsor and other key stakeholders should receive regular reports—either formally or informally—on the status of the project. In addition, the establishment of regular meeting times, during which the project manager can receive updates from the individuals accountable for the completion of each action step, will help to identify and resolve any problems before deadlines are missed. Clients of ours have used one of several available implementation-planning software packages, as well as e-mail, Intranet, and Internet applications to make this task easier. Whatever your method, regular communication will help reduce the likelihood of the project becoming stalled or derailed.

Exhibit 3.4 Potential Problem Analysis Worksheet

Potential Problems	P / I (H-M-L)		Likely Causes	Actions	
				Preventive	Contingent
1. Poor turnout for focus groups	H	M	• Conflicting priorities • Not perceived as important	• Check dates to ensure no conflict • Invite maximum number of participants • Have senior manager send confirmation letter	• Build in time to schedule additional focus groups if necessary
2. Too many one-on-one interviews for the available time frame and resources	M	H	• Too few project team members • Deadline too tight	• Add people to team • Spread due dates by two weeks	
3. Interim model not completed in time	M	H	• Unable to agree on competencies • Poor quality data collected	• Review interview questions • Practice interview • Extend due date	
4. People do not receive notice for focus groups or one-on-one interviews	M	H	• Incorrect E-mail addresses • Do not check E-mail • Treat as low priority	• Have senior manager send notice • Follow up with voice mail	• Identify alternate dates to use to reschedule

P = Probability   I = Impact
H = High, M = Medium, L = Low

Step Four: Identify Individuals at Various Performance Levels

Competency models describe how successful people carry out their work. When developing a model, therefore, you must first determine what successful performance (such as job outputs or results) looks like and then differentiate the behavior of successful performers from that of those who are less effective. But what succeeds varies between organizations and between roles. For example, performance criteria for managers could include quantitative factors, such as revenue levels, profitability, and employee turnover of the manager's work unit, and qualitative factors, such as employee morale, team satisfaction, and attention to development opportunities.

Once an agreement on performance criteria is reached, you must create interviewing and observation pools by identifying individuals who meet, exceed, or fall below expectations. This step can be challenging if no system is in place to measure or collect information about the performance indicators on an individual or work-unit level. In this case, consider using alternate methods such as performance appraisals, ratings of effectiveness from direct reports and colleagues, and input from a panel of informed judges. These are reasonable alternatives, but a less subjective approach is preferred whenever possible.

The quality of the performance criteria is particularly important because they serve as the foundation for many other steps: they help you develop interview questions that best reveal the relevant behaviors, offer a useful measurement tool when analyzing the information gathered from incumbents, and serve as the basis for validating the model to ensure that the people who have or use the identified competencies actually demonstrate successful performance.

Pitfalls to Avoid

From our many years of experience with hundreds of clients, we have seen organizations encounter a variety of pitfalls during the process of developing competency models. Following are some of the most common problems we have seen.

Developing the Competency Model in a Vacuum

This pitfall relates to a lack of context. Understanding the business need driving the project and the environment in which the job or jobs in question are performed is essential to provide focus for the effort. Identifying the key success factors for a specific job or role requires an idea of the deliverables expected from incumbents and the constraints and demands presented by their work environment. For example, how would the business environment of a salesperson dealing with commodity products in a stable industry compare to that of a salesperson dealing with specialty products in a turbulent marketplace? What are the implications of this environment for the behaviors that exemplify customer focus? Understanding the business context is essential for the competency model to reflect the unique aspects of the position in a given organization.

Changing Objectives in Midstream

Changing objectives during the development of the competency model could compromise the usefulness of the collected data or render it totally inappropriate. Understanding how the model will be used—for selection, training and development, performance appraisal, succession planning, or some combination of these—is a critical component for determining who to include in the process and what information to focus on and retain during the data collection phase.

Within each HRM system, the methods of incorporating competency models vary. For example, a competency-based selection system may include a list of interview questions designed to help the interviewer determine if a candidate possesses the relevant competencies. A selection or appraisal system may employ a continuum of unacceptable to acceptable behaviors illustrating the degree to which the relevant competency is being demonstrated. In Chapter Six, we discuss in more detail the various applications of competency models in HRM systems. Knowing the application in advance will provide focus for the information-gathering portion of the project and ensure that the relevant behavior examples are sought out and captured.

Concluding Remarks

Following the steps outlined in this chapter will help ensure the following:

- Your project objectives and scope are linked to a business need.
- Goals and standards are in place to guide and measure successful completion of the project.
- The project plan clearly outlines the necessary steps for successful development of a competency model.
- The impact of potential problems will be minimized through preventive and contingent actions.
- Established benchmarks provide the criteria to measure successful performance during the data collection and analysis processes.

In the next chapter, we examine the data collection and analysis processes for developing a competency model from scratch.

Chapter Four

Developing a Competency Model from Scratch

In this chapter, we discuss the four steps for collecting and analyzing data when developing a competency model from scratch:

1. Determine data collection methodology
2. Conduct interviews and focus groups
3. Perform job observations
4. Analyze data and develop an interim competency model

Although the recommended methodology for these steps is quite straightforward, ensuring the accuracy and usefulness of the information collected is a bit more challenging. As you will see, the processes of data collection and data analysis are intertwined. While you are collecting data, you are also formulating and testing assumptions and ideas about the key factors required for success in the role or organization. The challenge is to maintain a balance between the two activities and allow each to drive the other in equal measure.

Step One: Determine Data Collection Methodology

The purpose of data collection is to learn about critical incidents and stories that reflect effective performance of the job or role targeted in the study.

Decide Who You Will Interview

The size and quality of your interview pool at this early stage are important considerations to ensure the collection of useful and representative data. In an ideal world you would try to include everyone in the role or position under consideration. If that is not feasible due to practical considerations such as a large population of job incumbents or time and budget constraints, you may substitute a sampling that is statistically representative of the population in question. The guidelines in Exhibit 4.1 will help you in determining a statistically valid sample size. For some organizations, these guidelines may be somewhat restrictive. Although the sample is sufficient for developing the interim competency model, we strongly advise involving a wider audience during the refinement and validation stages of the process. Techniques for doing that will be discussed in Chapter Five.

The second consideration, the quality of the interview pool, is more challenging, as there are no charts to help guide your decision. Here your objective is to ensure that the sample truly represents the entire population, including a mix of geography, tenure in the job, gender, age, level (if appropriate), and performance (exceeds, meets, and falls below performance expectations).

Some competency model studies also include informed observers in the interview pool. Individuals who observe the incumbent in his or her role—bosses, direct reports, colleagues, and, when appropriate, customers—can provide additional insight and perspective.

Determine Data Collection Format

The two methods for collecting data are one-on-one interviews and focus groups. One-on-one interviews may be conducted either over the telephone or face to face. Ideally, focus groups should comprise five to nine people and be run by a trained facilitator. A group larger than nine makes it difficult for everyone to get "air time." Fewer than five people may not allow for enough give-and-take among

Exhibit 4.1 Table for Determining
Sample Size from a Given Population

N	S	N	S	N	S
10	10	220	140	1,200	291
15	14	230	144	1,300	297
20	19	240	148	1,400	302
25	24	250	152	1,500	306
30	28	260	155	1,600	310
35	32	270	159	1,700	313
40	36	280	162	1,800	317
45	40	290	165	1,900	320
50	44	300	169	2,000	322
55	48	320	175	2,200	327
60	52	340	181	2,400	331
65	56	360	186	2,600	335
70	59	380	191	2,800	338
75	63	400	196	3,000	341
80	66	420	201	3,500	346
85	70	440	205	4,000	351
90	73	460	210	4,500	354
95	76	480	214	5,000	357
100	80	500	217	6,000	361
110	86	550	226	7,000	364
120	92	600	234	8,000	367
130	97	650	242	9,000	368
140	103	700	248	10,000	370
150	108	750	260	15,000	375
160	113	800	265	20,000	377
170	118	850	269	30,000	379
180	123	900	274	40,000	380
190	127	950	278	50,000	381
200	132	1000	285	75,000	382
210	136	1100	288	1,000,000	384

Note: N is any complete group (population), S is sample size.

Source: Krejcie and Morgan, 1970.

group members and does not take full advantage of the potential time and cost savings this method can offer.

We recommend beginning the competency model study with one-on-one interviews. This format is most effective for gathering detailed information about the work environment—the daily issues and challenges faced by people holding the job—and the competencies demonstrated by people when carrying out their work. This data will also provide a context that interviewers can use to solicit input from a wider audience in the latter stages of the study.

Both types of data collection methods help lay the groundwork for building commitment and enthusiasm for the results of the study. By involving people early in the process, you increase the likelihood that they will buy in to the findings and the decisions about how the results will be used.

Organizations facing time or budget constraints may forgo the one-on-one interviews and use focus groups at this initial stage; however, they should be aware of the trade-offs of this choice. The pros and cons of each method are outlined in Exhibit 4.2.

A sample letter and list of questions for one-on-one interviews and focus groups are shown in Exhibit 4.3. This list reflects the range of questions we have used during interviews. We suggest you select the ones you feel would be most appropriate for the job or role in question, or you may use our list as a springboard to develop your own set.

Choose Data Recording Methods

The quality of data analysis and the overall success of the competency model depend on an accurate recollection and reflection of the incumbent's point of view. As we've seen, a competency model is intended to determine not only the skills and knowledge required for successful performance, but the characteristics or manner with which effective people perform their work. It is critical to capture the interviewee's comments completely and in his or her own words to identify the "how" of performance. There are three options for recording the information that will increase the likelihood of accu-

**Exhibit 4.2 Pros and Cons of
One-on-One Interviews and Focus Groups**

One-on-One Interview	Focus Group
Pros:	Pros:
• Encourages frank observations from incumbent	• Offers the opportunity to collect the perceptions of a greater number of people in an efficient manner
• Allows interviewer to probe for additional detail	• Dynamics of group discussion can solicit rich and sometimes unexpected information about the competencies required to succeed on the job
• Eases people's concerns about confidentiality	
• Savvy observers may provide context on role and organization	
Cons:	Cons:
• Conducting enough interviews to collect sufficient data can be time-consuming and costly	• A trained facilitator is required
	• Participants may be less likely to be candid in front of their peers
	• Quality of data may be compromised by a "group-think" mentality
	• Less opportunity exists to probe for further detail
	• A great deal of effort is required to organize and schedule

rately collecting the interviewee's comments and their meaning and intent: taping the interviews, using two interviewers (one to record comments), and extensive note taking by one interviewer.

Taping the Interviews. Accuracy and completeness are the primary advantages of this approach. Not only does it capture people's exact words, but you also have the benefit of being able to hear their tone of voice (this is particularly useful if a comment was made sarcastically or in jest). The main downside is the time required to review the tapes. Reviewing and documenting the findings of an hour-long interview can take two to three hours. Transcribing the tapes is a

Exhibit 4.3 Sample Letter for Interviews and Focus Groups and Sample Questions

As you know from a discussion with (name of person's manager or name of HR manager), Manus is working with (name of the organization) to develop a competency model for (name of position or level in the organization).

The purpose of this interview is to gain a better understanding of the nature of the work, the issues that are faced day to day, and specific behaviors that are used by (name of position or level in the organization).

(Name of interviewer), a senior consultant at Manus, will speak with you individually by phone/meet with you face to face. The interview will take about sixty minutes of your time, and your individual responses will be kept confidential. Your input will be combined with input from other participants in this effort. Following is a list of questions that will be covered in the interview.

(This list should be pared down to reflect the specific objectives of the user.)

Nature of the Work
- What is your role, and what are your key responsibilities?
- How do you typically spend your time?
- What are the primary challenges you will face in the next six to twelve months? What are some of the obstacles to meeting those challenges?
- What issues and challenges do you face day to day?
- In order to get your work done, which functions or departments do you need to involve and work closely with?

Work-Related Competencies
- Describe a problem you worked on that was resolved or handled successfully. What did you do? Why?
- Describe a problem you worked on that was resolved or handled unsuccessfully or poorly. What did you do? Why?
- Describe one of the more frustrating problems or situations you have encountered. What happened? How did you resolve it?
- Provide an example of something you have done that exemplifies a positive contribution of an effective (name of position or level).
- What are some of the factors that can limit success for people in your position?
- What are some of the behaviors or skills currently being used by people in this position (or level) that must be maintained to be successful? Why?
- What are some of the behaviors or skills that need to be changed and/or that are currently weak? Why? How can they be enhanced?

**Exhibit 4.3 Sample Letter for Interviews
and Focus Groups and Sample Questions, cont'd.**

If focus groups are used during the early stages of the data collection process, the questions could include:

- What are the key responsibilities of the (name of position) professionals in your organization?

- Describe a product or service provided by your organization to your customers that exemplifies "world class" (that is, is perceived as value-added, is innovative, and the like). What skills and/or knowledge are required to provide these products and services?

- Describe a recent problem you had with a (client, customer, colleague, boss, supplier) that was successfully resolved. Why did this end successfully?

- Describe a recent problem you had with a (client, customer, colleague, boss, supplier) that was not successfully resolved. Why did this end unsuccessfully?

- What behaviors distinguish the more successful from the less successful (name of position) in your organization?

- What is the primary challenge the (name of position) faces? What are the skills, knowledge, and characteristics that need to be developed to meet that challenge?

---

viable option, although it can also be time-consuming as well as costly. The willingness of interviewers to be taped is another consideration. However, if your objective is to achieve a high degree of accuracy and completeness, taping is the best option.

Using Two Interviewers. In this approach, one person leads the interview and directs the questioning while the second person records the interviewee's comments exactly as they are given. This method allows the interviewer to establish rapport with the interviewee, listen effectively, and probe for specifics without the distraction of taking notes. It also allows the "recorder" to begin coding comments as they are provided, facilitating the first step of the analysis phase: identifying themes and patterns. Although this approach does increase the accuracy and completeness with which the interviewee's comments are recorded, it is fairly labor-intensive.

Extensive Note Taking by Interviewer.   In our experience, having the interviewer take extensive notes is the most common approach. This method is more cost-effective than the others but does not allow for the same degree of accuracy and completeness. To be completely effective, it requires the interviewer to simultaneously facilitate the interview, listen, and take complete notes. Individuals with interviewing experience, personal knowledge of the particular position and role, as well as an understanding of how the information will be used and what the final product will look like will help increase the quality of data recorded with this method. Because the other methods compensate for a lack of interviewing experience, they may be a better option when using novice interviewers.

No matter which method you select, we recommend that interviewers agree on the format that will be used to record notes and share information. A consistent framework provides some discipline in capturing data and ultimately speeds up the analysis process.

Step Two: Collect Data

Ideally, the interview should last about ninety minutes. In reality, however, people are generally unwilling to schedule more than forty-five to sixty minutes out of their day. To make the best use of this time, provide the interviewee ahead of time with background on the project and the interviewer. Providing a preliminary set of questions in addition will encourage the interviewee to prepare and help to ensure that the discussion is focused and succinct.

Using the following guidelines will increase the likelihood that the time allotted for the interview is used effectively and that the data collected is of high quality.

Use Open-Ended Questions

Open-ended questions (for example, "What did you do when your competition introduced its new product?") allow the interviewee to respond in a full and complete manner. A closed question (for example, "Did you react quickly when your competitor introduced its new product?"), one that can be answered with a yes or no, only allows the interviewee to confirm or refute the interviewer's assumptions and is best used to clarify a given answer. Open-ended questions are more likely to capture the respondent's perceptions about the role or position in his or her own words.

Ask for Stories and Examples

The objective of the interview is to elicit detailed conversation from the interviewees regarding what they do, how they do it, and why they do it. The open-ended question should encourage the interviewee to relate a story or example that covers a range of behaviors, skills, and characteristics. Questions such as "What skills are required to achieve your business objectives?" or "How would you handle this hypothetical situation?" are unlikely to solicit the kind of detailed responses that are drawn from personal experiences. Instead, ask interviewees to describe how they have handled specific, real, work-related situations: "Describe a difficult problem you've faced and how you handled it" or "Tell me about the last time your division beat (lost to) the competition. How did it occur and what was your role in the outcome?" These types of open-ended queries encourage the incumbent to offer detailed stories that capture a range of competencies.

Probe for Specifics

The interviewer should not hesitate to probe for additional information when the interviewee responds with a generality or is unclear. For example, if the interviewee comments that he or she "believed the opportunity was apparent" or "did not take immediate action because the time was not right," the interviewer should ask follow-up questions to uncover the thought processes behind these conclusions.

The interviewer's job is to understand the specific behaviors used to resolve a situation or take advantage of an opportunity, and why those behaviors were selected. These behaviors must be captured during the interview in order to identify the relevant skills, knowledge, or characteristics without making assumptions or as-signing motives. Haphazard interpretations that are not firmly based in a respondent's comments will certainly cloud and contaminate the findings.

Avoid Leading or Directing the Interviewee

Interviewers may unwittingly direct the interviewee's responses in two ways. First, leading questions or statements ("What role did your perseverance play in the resolution of that problem? Tell me about how the ability to work with a diverse population helped you succeed") or a forced- or multiple-choice question ("How did you handle that problem? Did you call a meeting of the entire team or meet with the members one on one?") point interviewees toward a specific response that they might not have considered without prompting. Second, interviewers may unintentionally guide the in-terviewee toward specific answers through their own empathetic or judgmental responses. Comments such as, "That must have been terrible for you" or "Why would you do something like that?" indi-cate the interviewer's bias and provide cues to the perceptive inter-viewee about what answers are expected or preferred.

Establish a Comfortable, Open Environment

Making people feel at ease during the first few minutes of the meet-ing will increase the likelihood that they will speak freely and not self-edit their comments. A comfortable, open environment can be established through these simple steps: begin with a few words of wel-come; express appreciation for the person's willingness to take time out from their busy work schedules; have people introduce them-selves; review the objectives and agenda for the meeting; and tell the person how the information gathered during the session will be used.

Let the Interviewee Talk

The interviewees should do at least 90 percent of the talking. The interviewer's opinion about the competencies in question is not important at this point, nor is it necessary to provide stories about the difficulties of the project or personal experiences. The role of the interviewer is to encourage participation, record people's comments, and ensure that the agenda is covered on schedule.

The following two points are for focus groups specifically.

Have an Agenda and Stick to It

To ensure consistency of data collection, the interviewer must make sure that all the questions are covered in the time allotted. The management of the meeting, however, does not need to be heavy-handed, nor should the achievement of the task outweigh the objective of eliciting quality feedback and information from the group. The interviewer must balance maintaining an open, flexible environment with time management concerns.

Ensure That Everyone Participates

The primary objective of the focus group's facilitator is to ensure that everyone has a chance to express a point of view. It is important not to let one or two people dominate the conversation. If individuals are not engaged, the facilitator should ask them for their opinion or direct a question toward them, allowing them to be the first to speak.

During focus group meetings, differing points of view should be encouraged. People should also be made to feel comfortable disagreeing with each other's comments. In these situations, the facilitator should paraphrase the various viewpoints and highlight the value in each comment to decrease the likelihood of the conversation disintegrating into a protracted debate.

Step Three: Direct Observation of Incumbents

The interview, although it can be an important source of data for your competency study, has some flaws. What people say they do and what they actually do sometimes differ, as they may describe their behavior in terms of some ideal or expected response. Additionally, people may be less aware of the components or motivations behind behaviors that are based on good practice or experience and will therefore have difficulty describing them. Interviews, however, remain useful for eliciting stories about job behaviors that are often rich with contextual information about the conditions that either support or inhibit success.

Direct observation of incumbents on the job offers a reality check against the information gathered during the interviews. Spending a full or half day with someone and observing what the person actually does enables you to weed out idealized reports to create a more realistic picture of effective job behaviors.

We suggest observing at least three people who have not been previously interviewed from each performance category—exceeds, meets, and falls below criteria—to ensure the inclusion of a range of on-the-job behaviors. Similar to the interviewing process, however, the more observations you are able to perform, the richer your data will be.

It is important that the observation take place during a typical day; that is, the person being observed should not plan anything special or unusual for the day of observation. One potential problem, as with any study of this type, is that the mere presence of the observer changes the environment and the behavior of the person being observed; therefore, the observer should try to be as unobtrusive as possible. The observer should sit away from the main interaction (but close enough to hear the conversation), refrain from making eye contact with the incumbent or others present, and be careful not to communicate inappropriate cues through body language (such as raised eyebrows, heavy sighs, or slumping in the chair). In our experience, incumbents are usually very aware of being observed early in the day, but as they become caught up in daily activities, their self-consciousness lessens.

Exhibit 4.4 provides an example of a typical agenda for a "day-in-the-life" observation. Notice that we also take advantage of the opportunity to interview the incumbent and gather additional data.

Exhibit 4.4 Day-in-the-Life Observation Format

TO: Name of person to be observed

FROM: Observer

SUBJECT: "Day-in-the-life" observation

Manus is working with (name of organization) to develop a competency model that will pinpoint and refine the critical skills and behaviors needed to succeed as a (name of position or role). To help accomplish this objective, we will be conducting a "day-in-the-life" observation to gain a better understanding of your work environment and the demands of your position.

I will be visiting with you to observe your typical working day. Please do not plan anything special or out of the ordinary. It is important that we observe a typical day, whatever that might include. The observation will last about six hours. Following is the format you may expect:

First 30–45 Minutes—Introduction

- Tell us what we are about to see—What are you working on? What activities have you planned?

- How long have you been a (name of position or role)? What are the greatest challenges to your success?

- What contributes to the success of a (name of position or role) at (name of organization) now? What do you expect will contribute to the success of a (name of position or role) at (name of organization) in the future?

- What do you like most about your job? Least?

Next Four Hours—Observation

- Unobtrusive observation of you in your working environment

Last 30–45 Minutes—Review and Questions

- Is this typical of how you spend your time?

- How do your best/worst interactions differ from what we have seen?

- Describe any key activities you perform that we haven't been able to observe today.

If you have any questions or concerns prior to the observation, please do not hesitate to contact me at (insert e-mail or phone number).

Step Four: Develop an Interim Competency Model

This step involves examining the raw data collected during the interviews, focus groups, and day-in-the-life observations for themes and patterns, which are then analyzed to identify relevant competencies. Here you also begin looking for differences in the behavior of exceptional and standard performers. The analysis will result in a preliminary list of the skills, knowledge, and characteristics required by the job, referred to as an "interim competency model." This model will be used as the basis for additional data collection and will be circulated to a wider audience of stakeholders and incumbents for further refinement.

Reviewing the raw data to identify the competencies required to succeed in a particular job or role is as much art as science. For the science of it, we provide process steps and guidelines to help ensure that the result of your work is based on a rigorous and proven methodology. To provide insight into the art of it, we use our own experience and that of other practitioners. There is, however, no substitute for on-the-job experience. Practice, after all, makes perfect.

Identification of Themes and Patterns: Individual Work

At this stage of competency model development, the interviewer becomes a data analyst who combs through the information gathered during the interviews conducted and the observations made to identify common themes and patterns. The process involves three steps: isolating comments made by the interviewees that reflect specific skills, knowledge, and characteristics; grouping them; and assigning a name to each group. Often themes and patterns only begin to emerge after sifting through the data numerous times. Practice and prior experience in developing competency models can expedite this, but the less experienced person may benefit from using one of the two following approaches.

Start with a General Idea.   During the interview process, the interviewer will often hear repeated references to certain behaviors and skills, and patterns will emerge in the interviewees' descriptions of how they handled specific situations. These broad themes provide a starting point when reviewing the data in more detail. Specific quotes consistent with these themes can be grouped together as they are identified under the heading of a particular competency. If, however, there is insufficient data to support the original hypothesis, the theme must be abandoned or reshaped. Because additional themes frequently emerge during review of the material, data analysts should resist holding any preconceived notions about the expected outcome of their analysis and remain open to discovering new, unexpected findings.

Start with a Blank Slate.   In this approach, data analysts record any quote that refers to particular skills, knowledge, or characteristics. Once the list is complete, the frequency of similar comments is noted. Frequent similar comments may indicate a behavior that reflects a particular skill, knowledge, or characteristic. These various groups are then named to reflect the competency they represent and further developed through the process of organizing the quotes under the relevant competencies.

Following are some examples of individual data analyses from interviews conducted as part of a competency study for operations managers in a brokerage firm. They are based on real interviews but have been modified for length and to protect the confidentiality of the interviewee. Comments that support a frequently occurring theme or pattern are italicized; the relevant competency is added in parentheses. Additional potential competencies—which, after additional data analysis, may emerge as themes—are also shown for illustration. Note that the quotes are provided in the context of the complete comment. Context is critical to ensuring proper interpretation of the comment and the accurate identification of the competency. At this stage of analysis, we recommend that isolated quotes always be presented in context.

Example One

I don't really have a typical day, but inevitably *I spend a lot of time on my computer (computer literacy)* and *responding to various crisis situations (problem solving).* For instance, the other day one of my coworkers in another department called me in a panic. He had entered incorrect data on a particular client into his system, and as a result the client's loan fell through. *I helped him pinpoint the problem (problem solving), correct the data (computer literacy),* and gather all the background information he would need to meet with the client. I also *provided him with relevant information from my database (computer literacy),* then offered to help him resolve the crisis by joining him in the client meeting (supporting, customer focus). It's important that we own up to these kinds of problems and are quick to offer the client solutions (taking responsibility, customer focus). But it's even more *important to avoid computer data errors from the start (computer literacy)*—attention to detail and *a good understanding of the various computer systems are crucial (computer literacy) to this job.*

Example Two

One of my most challenging days with the organization occurred during year-end. I had only been working with the company for about six months, but there was an unbelievable amount of stress surrounding the end of the year. Not only that, but *it seemed like there were a million other issues and problems going on at the same time and I had to figure out what to focus on (handling multiple priorities).*

On this particular day, I had arrived early to work on a computer glitch, and the phone started ringing at 7 A.M. Unfortunately, the *interruptions continued throughout the day, making it nearly impossible to focus on my project (handling multiple priorities).* To make it worse, in the middle of the day, one of my assistants came to me with a serious client issue she thought I should handle right away. *This situation put me in a really difficult position because I knew that I had to fix the computer program before 5 P.M. It's always so hard to figure out when an emergency is really an emergency (handling multiple priorities).* Ultimately, I did handle the client's problem, which didn't turn out to be quite as serious as I thought, and I still had a little time to finish the other project. *I guess the flexibility to switch from one subject to the next is an important skill for this position (flexibility)*.

Example Three

To be effective, I have to be responsive, able to handle stress, and able to communicate clearly. Because of the pressure the whole team is under, this isn't easy. The brokers and sales assistants sometimes have little time to have a question answered or to get information from me. Sometimes, they can be very demanding because they need something done immediately. *It's easy to get frustrated and lose patience, but to be good at my job, I can't do that (patience, adaptability)*. I have to remember that I am a professional in a demanding work environment. *If I am trying to do ten things at once and someone throws one more thing on my plate, I have to remain calm, and remember that the whole team is doing their best (adaptability, patience)*. It's my job to help others when they need it, even before they think of asking for a hand. *We succeed or fail on our ability to work as a team (anticipating needs, teamwork)*.

Example Four

It's important for me to be *precise in my work*, especially when it gets busy. *If I give someone information that is wrong or the person misinterprets what I say, it could cost the company a lot of money (attention to detail, communication)*. *I need to think before I speak and keep my head when things are crazy (ability to handle stress)*. My situation can change from one minute to the next, and *I have to be able to respond to the changing demands without hesitation (adaptability)*. There are different personalities, and people react to stress in different ways. *If I can remember that it's up to me to read them and remain calm, then I help myself as well as the team (ability to handle stress, teamwork)*. This helps everyone remain focused on the job, not on personality conflicts.

Identification of Themes and Patterns: Project Team Meeting

Based on the individual analysis of these interviews, several competencies are beginning to emerge: computer literacy, problem solving, handling multiple priorities, adaptability, patience, ability to handle stress, and teamwork. This preliminary list of competencies and the supporting evidence for them is now ready for review with the other interviewers.

Frequently this work is accomplished during a series of meetings lasting a total of one to three days, depending on the complexity of the role or position under consideration and the consistency of the results arrived at by the individual analysis. As a result of this group review and discussion, some initial themes will receive further support, some will be reshaped, others will be eliminated, and an interim competency model will be produced.

The process for getting this group work done is similar to the one used for the individual work. Using one member's work as a starting point, the group discusses each competency and the supporting evidence, and everyone shares impressions and findings. During the discussion, the competency will either be confirmed (several other members of the group identify the same competency and have additional evidence), shaped (the beginning idea is fundamentally the same, but the emphasis or name of the competency changes—perhaps adaptability becomes flexibility, or self-confidence is redefined as self-sufficiency), or eliminated (there is not enough supporting evidence).

Depending on the composition of the group and the culture of the organization, these meetings can deteriorate into a presentation of entrenched points of view rather than a democratic sharing of perspectives. To ensure meaningful outcomes, however, the model should be shaped according to a variety of viewpoints. The following guidelines help to ensure that the group meetings run smoothly, everyone's time is used effectively, the diverse perspectives and opinions of the team are represented, and a high-quality product is generated.

Be Prepared. This is obvious but frequently ignored. Given the hectic nature and demanding workload of so many jobs today, people are sometimes unable to get to everything on their to-do list. However, if people are not prepared for meetings, valuable time is wasted in getting them up to speed or in trying to juggle busy calendars to reschedule, which threatens project deadlines. Therefore, each team member should always prepare for meetings by finishing individual analyses, being ready to discuss findings, and reviewing preliminary results produced by the other group members.

Use a Common Format to Present Findings and Supporting Evidence. Ideally, a group should agree in advance on a format to present its members' findings. This makes reviewing recommendations easier and allows people to compare "apples to apples." Some people may prefer to present interviewees' complete stories in order to have a fuller understanding of the interviewee's intent. Others may prefer a chart that includes the competency and a list of quotes that support the finding, as shown in Exhibit 4.5. And some may prefer a combination of the two—key phrases highlighted within full paragraphs to provide context, along with a chart that summarizes the findings.

Exhibit 4.5 Interim Competencies and Supporting Quotes

Competency	Supporting Quotes
Patience	"It's easy to get frustrated and lose patience, but to be good at my job, I can't do that."
	"If I am trying to do ten things at once and someone throws one more thing on my plate, I have to remain calm, and remember that the whole team is doing their best."
Handling multiple priorities	"Unfortunately, the interruptions continued throughout the day, making it nearly impossible to focus on my project. To make it worse, in the middle of the day one of my assistants came to me with a serious client issue she thought I should handle right away."
	"It seemed like there were a million other issues and problems going on at the same time, and I had to figure out what to focus on."

Demonstrate a Willingness to Be Influenced. In these types of discussions, an open mind and a willingness to be influenced can greatly enhance the result of the meeting. Using effective listening skills to check for understanding, presenting suggestions in a concise manner and supporting them with data, and being open to the ideas of others, even when they contradict your own, will increase the likelihood that any differences of opinion will lead to a productive discussion. These techniques also avoid the tendency to rely on compromise to break a stalemate. Compromise may move the conversation forward, but may not produce an outcome that accurately reflects the competencies required to succeed.

Keep the Client's Needs in Mind. The idea that the end users of the competency model depend on its accuracy and relevance may serve to increase team members' open-mindedness and their effective resolution of differences. If they remain focused on the client's objectives rather than a personal agenda, they may be more willing to entertain ideas different from their own.

Based on the individual and team analysis of information gathered from the interviews, an interim competency model can be developed. It is called an interim model because it is still a work in progress. The results must be further tested and refined with a broader population. For example, an interim model based on the comments in Exhibit 4.5 (and others not included there) might contain the suggestions listed in Exhibit 4.6.

Pitfalls to Avoid

When developing a competency model from scratch, individuals and project teams will benefit by avoiding the following pitfalls.

Lacking a Consistent Interview Protocol

Everyone who conducts interviews must use the same set of questions; the one variable in the process should be the interviewee. Interviewers should deviate from the predetermined set of questions

Exhibit 4.6 Interim Competency Model

Knowledge

Computer literacy

Successful operations managers know how to use proprietary computer systems for gathering information, analyzing data, tracking down problems, and communicating internally. In addition to knowing their own systems, they understand the systems that the operations department as a whole uses.

Business knowledge

The most successful operations managers have in-depth knowledge of how the firm is put together, including the key functions of various departments and key contacts within those departments. Also, they network appropriately to ensure that their information and understanding remain current.

Skills

Oral communication

Successful operations managers can speak with clients, brokers, and other staff members clearly, professionally, and respectfully and explain complicated issues and procedures simply and accurately. Their telephone manners (including grammar and diction) are impeccable, never reflecting impatience, frustration, or annoyance.

Prioritization/Time management

Successful operations managers allocate their time among their various responsibilities and prioritize issues quickly and appropriately to ensure that the needs of both internal and external clients are being met. They establish and maintain systems to ensure that pending issues and problems are quickly resolved and that time-sensitive issues are resolved according to daily deadlines. In addition, they can reprioritize their daily tasks to ensure that newly emerging urgent issues are resolved without losing sight of longer-term projects.

Problem solving

Successful operations managers determine the nature of a problem by asking appropriate questions, reviewing documentation, determining probable causes, and taking appropriate measures to resolve the issue in a timely manner. These measures might include communicating with the home office, obtaining additional information from the client, discussing the issue with the broker, changing information on the computer system, or working with branch staff to make changes or correct errors. In addition, they establish systems and procedures to ensure that a problem will not recur. They also take a great deal of satisfaction in helping others to solve problems.

Exhibit 4.6 Interim Competency Model, cont'd.

Listening

Successful operations managers are able to discern and respond to the feelings and underlying messages of clients, brokers, and others, pick out important information in oral communications, pay attention to orally presented facts and details, and appreciate feelings and concerns heard in conversation. Additionally, they must demonstrate to others that they have heard their concerns and are willing to take appropriate next steps.

Conflict management

Successful operations managers resolve disagreements with brokers, colleagues, and other staff members quickly and effectively, bringing a problem-solving attitude to conflicting approaches and priorities involving others. They also effectively mediate and resolve conflicts between others that might not otherwise involve him or her.

Ability

Ability to handle multiple tasks

Successful operations managers maintain focus on a task or project in the face of numerous incoming telephone calls, questions, and requests. When interrupted from their original task, they can judge whether to pursue the new issue or continue what they started. In addition, they are able to shift attention quickly to respond to the unexpected and simultaneously make progress on issues that range from the mundane the critical.

Attention to detail/Thoroughness

Successful operations managers complete forms accurately, spot omissions or errors in necessary documentation, and notice mistakes in the work of others, including brokers, associates in the branch and home office, clients, and client representatives such as attorneys and accountants. In addition, they are able to review large quantities of data and correspondence to spot errors, omissions, and inconsistencies.

Personal Characteristics

Adaptability/Flexibility

Successful operations managers can rearrange their schedules (work and personal) to meet the needs of the business, respond quickly to situations created by changes in market conditions, and adapt to the work styles of the brokers they support. In addition, they have a team orientation and are willing to proactively help out other sales assistants or brokers.

Exhibit 4.6 Interim Competency Model, cont'd.

Empathy

Successful operations managers truly enjoy dealing with people and are able to work with people of diverse styles and backgrounds. They understand the pressures facing brokers, operations personnel, sales assistants, and branch managers and respond appropriately. They display sensitivity to the needs and concerns of others and communicate with them tactfully even when they are unhappy.

Persistence/Follow-through

Successful operations managers see issues through to complete resolution. They check with the appropriate parties in the branch or home office and other personnel until they know that the issue or problem has been resolved completely. In addition, they find ways to overcome system or structural barriers that initially prevent them from solving problems immediately.

Stress tolerance

Successful operations managers are able to handle work pressures, uncertainty, and variability while maintaining effectiveness, poise, and an even temper. They thrive on variety and on dealing with unexpected events even when earlier plans are disrupted.

---

only when probing for more detail or specific examples. This helps ensure the quality of the data, makes the collation and reconciliation of findings easier, and increases the likelihood that comparable material is being analyzed and discussed.

Early on, you may discover that your interview protocol is not providing sufficiently rich and useful data. To avoid this, have group members conduct several pilot interviews and then fine-tune the interview questions and approach based on the group's collective experience. Be sure that everyone agrees before continuing.

Seeing What You Want to See

Personal biases and assumptions about what it takes to do a job effectively are difficult pitfalls to avoid. But such subjective interpretations of data are both unscientific and unethical. These biases can appear in two places. First, during data collection, interviewers may ask biased questions to elicit data in support of a personal hypothesis, focusing only on what they want to hear—the comments that support their assumptions versus those that contradict their beliefs. Second, during data analysis, bias can color interpretation of data; the interviewee's comments can be slanted to fit a preconceived model of effectiveness rather than allowing a more organic development of the model.

Having a sense of what you are looking for is useful in managing a large amount of information, but it is essential during data collection to remain open-minded and to be willing to recast assumptions and develop new hypotheses as data are collected. One way to do this is to involve several people in data collection and include the same people in data analysis. When the analysis is done in teams, individuals are required to support their findings with specific quotes and explanations. Comparing notes and looking for themes also makes it easier to move from assumptions to facts. In some projects, we asked people who did not participate in data collection to review raw data and identify themes and patterns. A naive resource can sometimes provide an objective view that people closer to the project may have lost.

If You've Seen One, You've Seen Them All

Just as interviewers may allow bias to interfere with their objectivity, they sometimes give verbal or influential interviewees too much weight. One can easily be influenced by a very glib or confident person, as if he or she represents the whole population, especially when interviews become tedious or repetitive. Conversely, if an interviewee is particularly entertaining, interviewers may overlook the step of probing for specific examples.

The job of the data gatherer is to treat each interaction as if it were the first, following the same interview protocol each time. We recommend scheduling a maximum of four interviews per day and allowing for a fifteen- to thirty-minute break between each to ensure that the interviewer remains fresh and focused.

Relying Solely on the Incumbent's Perception

Although the incumbent's perspective is critical to understanding what it takes to succeed in a particular job or role, self-reports and self-assessments can be flawed. People often report what they believe they should be doing rather than what they actually do. Nor are they always aware of their behavior and how it affects others. Or they may report what has worked for them even when not considered a best practice. For example, managers may report micromanaging or "kicking butt and taking names" as contributing to their success. Such actions may indeed work for them but be too idiosyncratic to be useful by a wider population.

To ensure the collection of data that reflect actual behavior, we suggest two tactics: observing the incumbent on the job during a typical work day and collecting information about his or her behavior from informed observers—direct reports, colleagues, boss, and internal and possibly external customers.

Concluding Remarks

As we've seen, the competencies required for effective data collection and analysis would be a long list indeed: patience, open-mindedness, diligence, cooperation, and attention to detail. The complex, iterative nature of the task can easily frustrate people. The support and feedback of a few individuals who are experienced in competency model development can help to mitigate some of this frustration.

This experience will also be helpful for the processes described in the next chapter: finalizing and validating the interim competency model.

Chapter Five

Finalizing and Validating Competency Models

At this point, we are still gathering and analyzing data. But the gathering is now more focused; we have a better idea of what we are looking for based on extensive interviews and analysis of that data. Still, we are far from ready to finalize the model. Our hypothesis needs to be further tested and refined, which requires involving a broader cross section of incumbents and stakeholders.

For the model to be used effectively, it must be shown to have *face validity* (that is, the competencies described in the model must make sense to those performing the job) and it must be validated as a predictor of successful performance (that is, the competencies must be demonstrated by the top performers in the job). Ensuring both types of validity is critical to gaining the endorsement of all levels of management and the target population. Four steps should be undertaken to ensure this:

1. Conduct focus groups, surveys, or both to test the model.
2. Analyze focus group and survey data and refine the model.
3. Validate the model to determine the correlation of the competencies with those of top performers.
4. Finalize the model.

Step One: Test the Competency Model

The purpose of this step is to test the accuracy and relevance of the interim model with a broader cross section of incumbents and stakeholders than that included in the initial data collection phase.

Circulating the model to a wider audience is important for two reasons. First, testing increases the likelihood that all relevant competencies have been captured, not just those expressed during the interviews. If the model will be used across functions or divisions or for the same position in several locations, the wider audience will also help uncover meaningful demographic or functional differences in the applicability of the model. For example, perhaps the competencies required in the southern region are slightly different from those called for in the west, or those required in marketing are irrelevant in engineering. Second, involving people helps build ownership and buy-in among those who will be affected by implementation of the final model.

Once the interim model is developed, two techniques—focus groups and surveys—can be used for collecting data to determine how well people currently in the position or role feel that the competencies reflect the skills, knowledge, abilities, and personal characteristics necessary to succeed. Both approaches are cost- and time-effective.

We recommend beginning with focus groups, which solicit detailed information about the interim competency model, and then using a survey to capture incumbent perspectives that have not been included in earlier data collection. The objective is to include as many people in the targeted position as possible. Additionally, soliciting the feedback of informed observers and key stakeholders will serve to provide additional insight regarding the model's relevance to the role in question. Involving them will also help generate the support necessary to successfully integrate the model into HRM systems.

Because a survey is the most efficient way to capture data from a wide audience, you may decide to use it instead of focus groups for practical reasons of time, budget, and the geographic distribution of incumbents.

The pros and cons of each method (some regarding focus groups have been previously mentioned) are outlined in Exhibit 5.1.

Exhibit 5.1 Pros and Cons of Surveys and Focus Groups

Surveys	*Focus Groups*
Pros:	Pros:
• Most efficient and simple method of collecting data from a large number of people	• Can collect the perceptions of many people efficiently
• Easy to administer	• Because of the dynamics of group discussion, can solicit rich and sometimes unexpected information
• Less disruptive of day-to-day activities	• Offers (limited) opportunity to probe for additional detail
• Generates quantitative data which will facilitate analysis	
• Confidentiality encourages candid replies	
Cons:	Cons:
• Does not allow for flexible responses	• Requires a trained facilitator to administer
• Offers no opportunity to probe for additional detail	• Data gathered are qualitative and thus more difficult to analyze
	• Participants are less likely to be candid in front of their peers
	• Quality of data may be compromised by a "group-think" mentality
	• Requires a great deal of effort to organize and schedule

Survey Method

When using surveys, the interim competency model is converted into a checklist. Respondents are asked to rate the relevance of each competency to the effective performance of their jobs. Sometimes people are also asked how frequently they currently use a competency. Exhibit 5.2 shows one section of a typical survey used to collect additional information about competencies for a finance professional.

Exhibit 5.2 Sample Competency Model Survey for a Finance Professional

Using this scale, rate the importance of each competency.

(4) Absolutely essential

(3) Essential

(2) Useful but not essential

(1) Unnecessary

Rating

Applies Knowledge of Financial Systems

- Knows the sources of information needed to get the work done   _____

- Understands the capabilities of the relevant financial systems in other parts of the organization   _____

- Understands how different financial systems interact with each other   _____

Acts as a Partner with the Business Units

- Understands and interprets the needs, issues, and interests of internal customers/business units   _____

- Provides objective and balanced value-added analysis for internal customers   _____

- Understands internal customer processes and procedures for capturing and consolidating data   _____

- Recommends/requests changes and/or enhancements in the processes and procedures of internal customers   _____

Takes Initiative

- Plans how to eliminate unnecessary actions and procedures in order to improve efficiency   _____

- Seeks answers to questions that enable solving a problem or completing a task   _____

- Anticipates potential problems or difficult situations and develops alternatives   _____

- Creates contingency plans in case the initial approach to a project or problem doesn't work   _____

- Proposes new and innovative approaches for dealing with problems or process improvements   _____

Focus Groups

These should be run by facilitators according to the guidelines described in Chapter Four for collecting initial data. In addition, make sure that attendees understand ahead of time what is expected of them and that they come prepared to discuss the competency model and to offer suggestions. Exhibit 5.3 shows a sample letter and interview questions that can be used to prepare them.

Exhibit 5.3 Sample Focus Group Information Letter

TO: Focus Group Participants
FROM: Project Coordinator
SUBJECT: Competency Model Focus Group

Thank you for taking the time to participate in a focus group for continuing research on the development of the competency model for [name of organization]. Competency models are used to establish the criteria (skills, knowledge, behaviors) for performance management and as a basis for establishing a curriculum that will address the organization's specific training and development needs.

The focus-group session will be held on [date] at [time] at [location]. We will ask you to review our findings to date and discuss how the current model applies to your role at [name of organization]. Attached you will find a draft of the competency model. To ensure that we use our time together most effectively, we would appreciate it if you could review the model and be prepared to discuss the following:

- To what extent does the model describe the most important aspects of your work?
- To what extent do the behaviors in each category accurately describe your work?
- To what extent are the categories clear and complete? What would you add? What would you change? Why?
- What ideas do you have about categories that could be added to make the model more applicable to your area of [name of organization]? Why?
- How well does the title of each category describe the behavior examples? Does it sufficiently capture the intent?

We look forward to seeing you on [date]. In the meantime, please do not hesitate to call me if you have any questions.

Step Two: Analyze the New Data and Refine the Model

New data from the survey or focus groups will enable you to determine if your assumptions about needed competencies are shared by most incumbents and informed observers. You can now clean up the model by eliminating items considered unimportant and by adding or modifying items viewed as more relevant.

Analyzing Survey Data

Analyze this data to determine which interim competencies are perceived as most essential. The process should uncover significant differences among groups of respondents. For example, do managers rate a particular competency as more relevant than do nonmanagers?

Exhibit 5.4 illustrates the simplest approach to this stage of analysis, using average scores and frequency distributions. A more complex analysis that uses sophisticated statistical techniques (such as t-test, standard deviations, and one-way ANOVA) could also be used to help the competency model team draw its conclusions (see Exhibit 5.5). Although average scores, frequency of responses, and median scores assist the team in eyeballing levels of agreement between groups, the more sophisticated analysis increases your confidence in the final conclusions. (For a more complete explanation of these statistical techniques, please refer to Welkowitz, Ewen, and Cohen, 1982.)

Analyzing Focus Group Data

The process for analyzing these data is similar to the one described in the previous chapter for analyzing one-on-one data: the facilitator sorts through attendee responses to identify common themes and prepares these findings for the project team's review. Here are some questions and responses collected during the focus group session in that case.

Exhibit 5.4 Portion of Survey Data for Finance Professional: Average Scores and Frequency of Responses

Rating Scale:

(4) Absolutely essential

(3) Essential

(2) Useful but not essential

(1) Unnecessary

	Avg.	Frequency* 1&2	3&4
Applies Knowledge of Financial Systems			
• Knows the sources of information needed to get the work done	3.6	0	29
• Understands the capabilities of relevant financial systems in other parts of the organization	3.6	0	38
• Understands how different financial systems interact with each other	3.5	2	27
Acts as a Partner with the Business Units			
• Understands and interprets the needs, issues, and interests of internal customers/business units	3.3	2	36
• Provides objective and balanced value-added analysis for internal customers	3.4	2	27
• Understands internal customer processes and procedures for capturing and consolidating data	3.3	5	33
• Recommends/requests changes and/or enhancements in the processes and procedures of internal customers	3.3	2	27
Takes Initiative			
• Plans how to eliminate unnecessary actions and procedures in order to improve efficiency	3.3	6	32
• Seeks answers to questions that enable solving a problem or completing a task	3.6	0	38
• Anticipates potential problems or difficult situations and develops alternatives	3.5	2	27
• Creates contingency plans in case the initial approach to a project or problem doesn't work	3.3	2	36
• Proposes new and innovative approaches for dealing with problems or process improvements	3.4	2	27

*Total number of responses varies due to some incomplete questionnaire responses.

How well does the title of each category describe the behaviors? Does it sufficiently capture the intent?

I am really pleased with the competencies that you came up with, but don't you think there are too many?

It's not as much priorities as it is just a lot of stuff to do. It's the ability to juggle the fifty new tasks that come up each day. Priorities are an issue, but just a part of a larger topic. The behaviors are accurate, but the title is somewhat misleading.

Business knowledge is such a broad category. Everyone in the business world needs business knowledge. What we really need is a specific knowledge of the trading systems that we use on a day-to-day basis. That is what is critical to success in this organization.

Describe the degree to which each behavior and competency category is important to your role.

Being adaptable and flexible is an absolutely essential part of my job. Each day there are new opportunities or problems that you need to react to and deal with appropriately.

There's a tendency in this business to be too tough and not supportive enough. People hesitate to spend extra time helping someone out if they have a difficult or stressful task or responsibility. Everyone is trying to be a lone ranger. I think that empathy is a critical competency in moving forward and building the type of environment and culture that we need.

Refining the Model

Based on qualitative data from the focus groups and on quantitative survey data, the project team refines the draft model to reflect the new information. Competencies may be added, deleted, or redefined. Behavior examples may be modified or expanded. For example, in our illustration from Chapter Four, "handle multiple priorities" might be changed to "handle multiple tasks," and "business knowledge" might be changed to "trading systems knowledge." "Empathy" might be deleted.

The final step in refining the model is to circulate it to a cross section of people who participated in the study. This ensures that you have captured the key elements and critical success factors of the job. This final test will determine if the competency model has strong face validity.

From Interviews to Refined Model: One Competency

To illustrate the evolution of a competency and the flow of the data analysis process, here is how one developed: the compound business of the Geon Company (see Chapter Two for a description of its business need).

One-on-One Interviews and Individual Analysis of Data. The interview guidelines and questions were developed by key stakeholders and Manus consultants familiar with the company's business issues and purpose for developing a competency model. The questions focused on areas that the project team felt would elicit information particularly relevant to the organization. Here is a selection of quotes that were provided for each key area of questions about the competency "communication."

> Typically, they are excellent communicators, and they continually talk about what quality is and what our priorities are. They are able to continually keep that message in front of people, and you know what direction they are going in. They have a real clarity and consistency of the messages.

> Good listening skills, and can make a person feel that what the person is saying is important even if they don't agree, and can challenge

people in a way that motivates them. Very good communication skills and they take the time to get out and talk to all levels in the organization.

Change or do differently? We need to be more open to different ideas. We have a lot of not-invented-here syndrome and it-never-worked-before attitude in just about every group. We need to explore old ideas again or new ideas we've never had before.

Communications. We struggle as an organization to communicate. This includes managers to each level and getting information we need to do our job from others.

Learning from our own mistakes and not repeating them is critical. We need to communicate this knowledge to others and get over our ego problems. We need to get over not being the only one who solves a problem.

The biggest resource issue we face right now is people. We need to prioritize the tasks we have before us and be sure everyone understands what to focus on to ensure the high-impact activities get people's time.

We have a tendency to think that everyone should know everything. We need to help people focus on what they need to know to do their job.

We need to make sure we keep getting out and communicating to our people. There is some fear about future changes and leaders need to get out and communicate what is going on so that people can understand what is happening and be productive, rather than get distracted.

People have to be ready to speak up, to pinpoint trouble areas before they become an emergency. Each and every person has to be aware when they are overloaded and speak up. You can't just absorb it and be macho.

We need continued communication and open information. We need healthy dialogue re: issues/conflict. This leads to unified goals and strategies. We need to learn from mistakes, share knowledge, and support each other.

Development of an Interim Model. The project team members met to review their individual findings. Communication was identified by each as a critical competency, and they drafted a definition that included key behaviors that illustrated what the team felt the interviewees meant by communication and what it looked like when used effectively. Here is the team's first draft.

Communication

Able to clearly and consistently communicate priorities. Provides others at all levels of the organization with the information they need to effectively handle critical issues. Keeps others informed about the progress being made on business and organization-wide initiatives. Promotes a feedback process where both good and bad news is leveraged for ongoing learning.

Focus Group Reaction, Recommendations, and Survey Results. The interim model was brought to ten focus groups of seven to nine people each and included in a survey that was distributed to an additional 125 people. Based on focus group and survey data the competency was modified to include behaviors that reflect the timely exchange of information, listening skills, open-mindedness, and following up. The survey data confirmed that communication was indeed a critical factor for success in the compound business at Geon, but no changes were made based solely on it. Rather, the definition of communication competency was refined to this (italics represent changes to the original):

Communication

Able to clearly and consistently communicate priorities. *Ensures timely exchange of information between teams/functions/departments.* Provides people at all levels of the organization with the information they need to effectively handle critical issues. Keeps others informed about the progress being made on business and organization-wide initiatives. *Listens attentively to the ideas, concerns, and opinions of others, and demonstrates understanding by paraphrasing or responding appropriately.* Promotes a feedback process where both good and bad news is leveraged for ongoing learning. *Is open-minded when approached with new ideas and opinions. Follows up to ensure that information and ideas are clearly understood.*

Step Three: Validate the Competency Model

By now the interim model has been tested and refined; it has been determined to have a high degree of face validity. The competency study may even have differentiated top performers from average performers to identify critical competencies. If the model is to be used for training and development only, face validity may be sufficient to ensure that the model contains the skills, knowledge, and characteristics required for success on the job. But if the model will be used as the basis for selection, appraisal, or compensation systems, the additional step of validating the model is highly recommended.

This step is often considered optional, but we think it essential; the further the model gets from creating awareness of individual strengths and weaknesses and the closer it gets to recommendations and decisions about how people should behave, the more important validation of the model becomes. If it is to be used in hiring decisions, you must know how well the competencies predict success. If it is to be used in performance appraisal decisions and recommendations, you must know how often the most effective managers use the competencies and when they correlate with measures of performance such as productivity, increases in sales or profit, employee satisfaction, and the like. This is especially true if the competencies are to be used to make decisions about compensation.

A validation study is not particularly complex, but it can be time-consuming and require specialized skills in data analysis. The necessary steps to set up and conduct the study include the following:

1. Converting the list of competencies into a 360-degree feedback questionnaire

2. Having a cross section of incumbents in each of the three performance groups—those who exceed, meet, and fall below performance criteria—identified at the beginning of the study distribute the questionnaires to direct reports, colleagues, the boss, and external customers, if appropriate

3. Analyzing the data

Converting Competencies into a 360-Degree Questionnaire

This can be straightforward if it was identified as part of the project plan from the beginning. Select four to six specific and observable behaviors that illustrate competency on the job. Examples can be gleaned from the definition of competency used during the refinement of the model and from interviews and focus groups. Arrange the behavioral items so that they illustrate each competency in a survey format. Here is part of a 360-degree questionnaire outlining the behavior of a person who exemplifies the competency of adaptability and flexibility.

1. Rearranges his or her schedule to meet the needs of the business

2. Responds quickly to situations created by changes in market conditions

3. Adapts to the working styles of the people he or she supports

4. Is willing to put work aside and proactively help others

A rating scale accompanying such a list allows bosses, direct reports, colleagues, and customers (if appropriate) to rate the importance of the competency, how often it has been used, and how often it should actually be used.

Distributing 360-Degree Questionnaires

Select at least eighty managers—fewer if the organization is small—who are above, at, and below the performance criteria developed during the first stage of the project (their performance-level estimates must be known by no one, including themselves). Each should have at least three direct reports and three colleagues to ensure enough data to work with and to produce statistically accurate results. Give each of them ten to fifteen paper or electronic questionnaires.

Instruct them to distribute the questionnaires to five to seven direct reports, five to seven colleagues, and all of their supervisors. The raters complete the questionnaire and return it. Sometimes a third party outside the organization is used to ensure confidentiality and anonymity and to perform the more complex statistical analyses.

Analyzing the Data

The scores are tabulated for each individual and analyzed for the strength of the relationship between the competencies and the aggregate ratings of the different performance groups. If there is a significant correlation between the competency and the high-performance group, the competency is said to have concurrent validity. Significant differences between competency scores of high performers and low performers are also considered. If there are weak relationships between a competency and the high-performance group, consider reviewing the clarity of the behavior descriptions. The soundness of the performance criterion used to select the groups could also explain the weak relationship. In this case, review the criterion to ensure it measures successful performance as objectively as possible.

An example of the data analysis to determine the validity of a competency model for sales associates at a mortgage bank is shown in Exhibit 5.5.

Exhibit 5.5 Sections of Sales Competency Validation Study

Data Analyses

The mean effectiveness ratings of each sales associate were used to separate the population into two groups: performers above the median and performers below the median.

Competency scores were compared between rater groups by using t-test and ANOVA comparisons with a significance cutoff of $p < .05$. A value of .05 means that there is a 5 percent (or one in twenty) probability that the difference found between the groups being compared is due to chance. Significance values less than or equal to .05 indicate that there is a significant difference between the groups.

Key Findings

• All competencies were rated between "very important" and "absolutely essential" by all rater groups.

• Customer ratings of the above-median group's use of each competency are significantly higher than their ratings of the below-median group. This supports the validity of the sales competency model for use with the company sales force.

• Sales managers and colleagues rated the above-median performers higher than the below-median performers on all competencies; differences were statistically significant for the following competencies:

  – Listening beyond product needs
  – Coordinating resources
  – Consultative problem solving
  – Engaging in self-appraisal and continuous learning
  – Providing quality service (significant for colleagues only)

Key Drivers of Sales Associate Effectiveness

A correlation analysis answered a question about which behaviors have the greatest impact on people's perception of a sales associate's effectiveness. The behaviors include the following:

• Engaging in self-appraisal and continuous learning

• Consultative problem solving

• Listening beyond product needs

Step Four: Finalize the Model

Using the analysis of 360-degree data, finalize the model by eliminating any categories or items that do not correlate with effectiveness. At this point, you can be highly confident that the competencies and their associated behaviors can be used as the basis for developing or enhancing tools used for human resource decision making.

Starting with an Existing Validated Competency Model

As discussed in Chapter Two, you may use an existing validated competency model as the starting point for developing a competency model for your organization. This off-the-shelf approach supplants extensive interviews and observations of incumbents on the job. It may save time on data collection and analysis and on validating a model you create, but the functions and roles appropriate for it are limited. Because it is generic and not developed with a specific job or position in mind, it may not address the technical skills and knowledge required for the job or position you are considering. Generic models are best suited for leadership and management roles that cut across several functions and for positions that require limited technical skills and knowledge.

It is still useful to begin by clarifying performance criteria for the work unit and the individual. Doing so is the basis for selecting one of the many validated competency models available in the marketplace. Exhibit 5.6 shows a sample from Compass, a validated model of leadership and management competencies we have developed. We frequently begin with this list of competencies, assemble the appropriate mix of competencies, and customize the behavior items to reflect the nature of the organization and the position we are working with.

You may find an existing validated competency model available in the form of a 360-degree questionnaire that will save you the

Exhibit 5.6 Selected Competencies from Compass: A Validated Model of Leadership and Management

Risk Taking

Taking calculated, prudent risks; experimenting with new approaches to discover if they will be successful; taking responsibility for making difficult decisions

Credibility

Keeping promises; honoring commitments; accepting responsibility for mistakes; being honest and truthful when communicating information; behaving consistently with espoused values

Strategic Thinking

Identifying the implications of social, economic, political, and global trends; showing an understanding of market conditions and customer needs; taking a long-term perspective on problems and opportunities; proposing innovative strategies that leverage the organization's competitive advantage

Customer Focus

Demonstrating a concern for the needs and expectations of customers and making them a high priority; maintaining contact with customers; using an understanding of customer needs as the basis for decision making and organizational action

Consulting

Checking with people before making changes that affect them; encouraging participation in decision making; allowing others to influence decisions

Influencing

Using techniques that appeal to reason, values, or emotion to generate enthusiasm for the work; committing to task objectives; complying with requests

Recognizing

Giving praise and showing appreciation to others for effective performance, significant achievements, and special contributions trouble of developing your own. The purpose of collecting 360-degree data is to determine which competencies differentiate superior performers from those who are only satisfactory.

The steps involved in using an existing competency model parallel those for refining and validating one developed from scratch:

1. Conduct focus groups and surveys to include a wider population and test the degree of relevance and importance to the job.
2. Analyze focus group and survey data and refine the model.
3. Correlate the competencies with those of top performers in your organization.
4. Finalize the model.

Shortcut Methods

Their scientific rigor increases the likelihood that the models already described predict success in a particular job or role, but we realize that some organizations may seek a simpler method. Following are some shortcuts for both methods of competency model development. Although they are intended to maintain the integrity of the process, they will not provide as much confidence in the final product as the more rigorous approaches. If, however, you are aware of the limitations and trade-offs and are willing to accept them, they may serve you well.

Starting from scratch, do the following:

1. Identify performance criteria for success in the job or role.
2. Interview incumbents and informed observers.
3. Develop an interim competency model by analyzing data for themes and patterns.
4. Conduct surveys or focus groups to include a wider population and test their degree of relevance and importance to the job.
5. Finalize the model.

A limitation of this method is that it depends on reports from the incumbent without verifying the data by observing behavior on the job. Nor is the final model analyzed beyond its face validity—people may believe that competencies are relevant and important to their job even when no evidence links the competencies to work unit or individual performance.

Starting with a validated competency model, conduct a short-cut by doing the following:

1. Identify performance criteria for success in the job or role.
2. Select a validated competency model from among those available in the marketplace.
3. Use a survey or focus group or both to test the degree of relevance and importance to the job in your organization.
4. Finalize the model.

If time and budget do not permit a complete study, we recommend starting with a validated competency model. This avoids many pitfalls and provides a greater degree of confidence that the competencies you are working with are in fact related to effective job performance.

Concluding Remarks

Although we emphasize the need for scientific rigor and the use of statistically accurate data when developing a competency model, experience has taught us that statistics alone cannot provide an accurate picture of what people need to do on the job to be successful. Nor is using only empirical data and incumbent comments on what they believe people should do on the job sufficient. Striking the correct balance between statistical techniques and practical considerations is critical for a high-quality result. Therefore, both aspects must be considered as the data are reviewed and analyzed to produce a competency model that accurately reflects what it takes to succeed in a job. To do that, it helps to consider the big picture—who the model is being developed for and how it will be used, not just the statistical results of a survey or set of interviews.

Developing a good competency model depends as much on the quality of the final product as on the belief that it is a useful human resource tool by those who will use it. The various methods of gathering feedback from incumbents, informed observers, and key stakeholders help by allowing these individuals to offer their input. Testing and validating the model also increases your confidence when using it to make human resource decisions. In the next chapter, we look at how to convert the competency model into a useable HRM tool.

Chapter Six

Integrating Competency Models into HRM Systems

After you develop the model, you face the challenge of integrating it into existing HRM systems. As we have discussed, it is important for key decision makers to agree on the eventual application of the model at the beginning of the project. Implementation will be much easier if you already have the support of those responsible for applying the model, as well as those who will be affected by it.

After a model has been developed, the next step is to make it usable by translating it into a format tailored to its purpose. Among 217 large North American companies that participated in an American Compensation study in 1996, 40 percent had competency-based human resource programs under development (O'Neill, 1996). Exhibit 6.1 summarizes the various ways a competency model can be put to use in HRM systems and briefly describes the form the model might take. (See Dubois, 1998, for twelve comprehensive case studies on the use of competency models in human resource practices.) Regardless of the application, the primary function of the tool you are creating is to provide a simple method for users to describe the competency, recognize when it is being used (or the potential for it to be used), and evaluate how well it is being used (or the potential for it to be used effectively).

Implementing a Competency-Based Selection System

Many organizations find that when they use competency models to select new employees, they encounter less resistance than when they use competency models in other HRM processes. Enhancing

**Exhibit 6.1 Format of Competency
Models for Each HRM System**

Use	Format
Selection	• Competency with definition • List of interview questions to elicit information about relevant behaviors • Interviewee rating form providing a continuum of unacceptable to acceptable behavior examples
Training and Development	• Three to six behavior examples for each competency that describes exceptional performance • Rating scale for frequency or effectiveness of competency • Rating scale of importance of the competency to current or future role • List of workshops or development experiences available for skill improvement
Performance Appraisal	• Description of three to five levels of effectiveness for each competency, from above standard to below standard • Checklist with specific behavior examples for each competency
Succession Planning	• Competency with description of behavior/ ability required to perform the job • Rating process to indicate current level of ability • Suggestions for how to develop competency

or modifying the selection system may seem more manageable than applying a model to appraisal and succession planning; managers at all levels are generally able to appreciate the benefits of using a competency model. Also, the impact of competency-based selection on the quality of new hires is easier to measure.

For one of our mortgage banking clients, the benefits were quickly recognized. Managers reported an immediate improvement in the quality of the interviews they conducted. They also reached agreement on hiring decisions more easily. Three months later, when the new hires were expected to have achieved specific performance objectives, the organization found that each had met or exceeded minimum expectations, unlike before the use of a competency-based system.

Thus we recommend starting with selection when implementing competency models. An early win and good word of mouth will make the use of competency models in other HRM systems that much easier. And if your overall objective is to link all HRM systems through the use of competency models, hiring is the logical place to start.

To implement a competency-based selection system, an organization needs the following:

1. A validated competency model that predicts success on the job

2. A set of interview questions that helps interviewers determine if a candidate has the required competencies or the potential to develop them

3. Interviewers with the training and experience to evaluate whether a candidate is competent or has the potential required for the job

4. Forms to record results and help compare and evaluate candidates

A Validated Competency Model

Using a validated competency model helps ensure that hiring deci-sions are based on criteria that specifically predict success on the job, rather than those that seem relevant to a particular interviewer. Given the costs associated with making poor selections—the cost of training, recruitment, and lower productivity—hiring based on criteria that have been proven relevant to performance offers great value.

Exhibit 6.2 shows a validated competency model used by orga-nizations that focus on business-to-business selling. Research con-ducted by Manus and MOHR (1997) has shown that salespeople who have the competencies listed in the exhibit tend to perform better on the job. When these competencies are used as the basis for interviewing and hiring salespeople, performance by new hires has been shown to improve, and turnover decreases.

A Library of Interview Questions

Once the competencies for effective performance have been iden-tified, an interviewer must determine if a job candidate possesses them or is able to develop them. To do this, ask them the right questions. Samples we developed for a sales assistant competency model are shown in Exhibit 6.3. These are part of a selection guide for managers, but you may recall that there is no simple relationship between questions and competencies; questions are designed to encourage candidates to talk about their current and past expe-riences and may address several competencies at once. In addition, it is possible to learn about personal characteristics and aptitudes using well-constructed questions.

Trained Interviewers

The skills of the job interviewer are important. He or she must be able to use the library of questions effectively, probe for specifics rather than generalities, and interpret responses in terms of the

Exhibit 6.2 Sales Competency Model

Skills

Basic selling skills

Establishes rapport, determines customer needs, relates benefits to product features, handles objectives, and closes

Strategic selling skills

Listens beyond product needs and establishes a vision of a customer-supplier relationship that supports the strategic direction of both organizations

Consulting skills

Involves others in decisions that will affect them, encourages participation of key stakeholders in problem solving, and develops breakthrough ideas and solutions

Problem-solving skills

Anticipates problems, invites ideas, distinguishes symptoms from causes, modifies proposals, and implements solutions

Knowledge

Financial analysis

Understands the financial impact of decisions on the customer, the customer's customer, and the organization

Market analysis

Understands market trends and the implications of those trends for the industry, customers, markets, and the competition

Business planning

Understands the factors that affect an industry's potential for profitability and growth and a company's competitive position, and how this information is used to determine the strategic direction and annual business plan for the company

Computer literacy

Has basic computer skills for application to marketing programs, including prospect lists, customer contacts, and relevant economic data

Business process improvement

Understands the relationship between different business processes and uses this knowledge to identify inefficiencies or problems and make recommendations to simplify and improve the process

Product knowledge

Possesses expertise related to the company's products and services as well as to other crucial aspects of the business

Exhibit 6.2   Sales Competency Model, cont'd.

Ability

Mental agility

Is able to deal with multiple issues and details, is alert, has the capacity to learn

Critical thinking

Possesses inductive and deductive thinking abilities, can draw conclusions from limited or related information, and proactively seeks relevant information

Quantitative reasoning

Is able to reason with, analyze, and draw conclusions from numbers; feels comfortable with quantitative data

Divergent thinking

Is able to see and think beyond the obvious and formulate original solutions

Personality

High endurance (longer selling cycle)

Is willing and able to put off immediate gratification and focus on another person's needs; is able to invest time and energy over a long period for a future benefit or reward

Achievement need

Measures self-worth and gains personal satisfaction from accomplishing personal and business objectives and achieving results

Reflectiveness

Is self-aware and understands how other people perceive him or her, thinks about the impact of words and behavior on others before acting, is not impulsive

Affiliation need

Has a desire to interact with others and, when doing so, projects warmth and relates well to a variety of people; wants to be liked and accepted by others

Assertiveness

Able to take command of face-to-face situations while displaying appropriate tact and diplomacy

Self-management

Can work independently for extended periods with minimal support and approval, takes initiative, is proactive, and takes ownership for personal success

Exhibit 6.3 Library of Selected Interview Questions

1. Describe a situation in which your workload was too heavy. How did you handle it?

2. Tell me about a time when you were trying to accomplish something and did not have ready access to the necessary resources. How did you get them?

3. Describe a situation in which you had to juggle more than one task. How did you sort them out? Which did you tackle first and why?

4. How do you typically organize your time?

5. Tell me about a time when your work plan wasn't helpful. What happened and how did you recover?

6. Tell me about a time when you had to deal with two people asking you to do work on different projects that required more than 100 percent of your time. How did you resolve the situation?

7. Give me an example of a time when you were unable to meet your goals. What did you do?

8. Describe a time when you delivered superior customer service. What were the circumstances? What did you do? How did the customer respond?

competencies. In addition, applying three key predictive principles helps the interviewer assess whether candidates have or can develop the relevant competencies:

1. Past behavior best predicts future behavior; people who use a competency once are likely to use it again.

2. People are consistent; if they use a competency in one situation, they will probably use it in another.

3. Predicting failure is easier than predicting success. Many factors contribute to success, but failure can be caused by deficiency in even a single competency.

Applying these principles when posing questions and probing for specifics increases an interviewer's ability to assess during a brief interview whether a candidate possesses competencies or can develop them. In light of the third predictive principle, interviewers should be trained to look for deficiencies, not just the competencies that fit with the job requirements. Identifying a candidate's strengths and assessing whether he or she has the proper background is relatively easy; more difficult is determining the factors that may hinder a candidate's success.

Interview Forms to Record Results

A standard format for collecting information about the interview increases the likelihood that facts and impressions about candidates are not forgotten or misrepresented with the passage of time. If there are multiple interviewers, it also ensures that they focus on identical selection criteria. An example of a job aid developed for the business-to-business sales competency model is shown in Exhibit 6.4. The aid allows interviewers to rate a candidate's demonstration of the relevant competencies as well as to cite behavioral examples to support their rating under the "Why" section.

Implementing a Competency-Based Training and Development System

As mentioned earlier, people are less likely to resist competency models in hiring new personnel than in performance management and succession planning. Similarly, few resist using competency models to enhance the relevance and effectiveness of training and development programs; many organizations have begun introducing competencies into these systems through 360-degree feedback questionnaires.

A 360-degree feedback questionnaire is similar to a competency model in that it contains a list of behaviors for effective performance. 360-degree feedback is now used in many training and development systems to create awareness of the need for change, to focus people on their strengths and development needs, to identify organizational development needs, and to monitor improvement in behavior on the job.

Exhibit 6.4 Interview Data Form

Rate the candidate for each competency (circle one number in each category):

Competency	Above Standard		Meets Standard		Below Standard
Communication Skills	5	4	3	2	1
	Always asks and answers questions clearly; displays good understanding of questions; demeanor is highly professional and friendly		Asks and answers most questions clearly; displays adequate understanding of questions; demeanor is generally professional and friendly		Questions and answers not clearly stated; often does not understand questions; demeanor is often unprofessional and unfriendly

Why? _____

_____

_____

Competency	Above Standard		Meets Standard		Below Standard
Basic Selling Skills	5	4	3	2	1
	Quickly establishes rapport; skillfully listens to identify customers' needs; relates benefits and product features to the buyer; handles objections well and is skilled at closing sales		Adequately establishes rapport; listens to identify customers' basic needs; can adequately relate benefits and product features to the buyer; adequately handles objections and closes sales		Slow to establish rapport; has difficulty identifying customers' needs; struggles to relate benefits and product features to buyers; is unskilled at handling objections and closing sales

Why? _____

_____

_____

Exhibit 6.4 Interview Data Form, cont'd.

Competency	Above Standard		Meets Standard		Below Standard
	5	4	3	2	1
Organizational Skills	Keeps flawless customer records and conducts timely customer follow-ups; consistently tracks progress toward sales targets and goals; pays strict attention to details; is very effective at managing time		Keeps adequate customer records; tracks progress toward sales targets and goals; pays attention to details; is somewhat effective at managing time		Is negligent in keeping customer records; does not adequately track sales progress, targets, or goals; is inattentive to details; is ineffective at managing time

Why? _____

_____

Competency	Above Standard		Meets Standard		Below Standard
	5	4	3	2	1
Customer Focus	Always operates with customers' best interests in mind; has a history of repeat business; exceeds customers' expectations		Usually keeps customers' best interests in mind; positions himself or herself for repeat business; strives for customer satisfaction		Often fails to act with customers' best interests in mind; positions himself or herself poorly for repeat business; often fails to achieve customer satisfaction

Why? _____

_____

Conflict Management

5	4	3	2	1
Has high level of skill resolving differences and reaching agreement by maintaining a problem-solving attitude		Has adequate skill resolving differences and reaching agreement by maintaining a problem-solving attitude		Has little skill resolving differences and reaching agreements and fails to adopt a problem-solving attitude

Why? _____

_____

_____

Product Knowledge

5	4	3	2	1
Has extensive knowledge of product or service features, benefits, and performance statistics; stays up to date on product or service information		Has basic understanding of product or service features, benefits, and performance statistics; is up to date on some product or service information		Is unfamiliar with product or service features, benefits, and performance statistics; is not up to date on product or service information

Why? _____

_____

_____

Increasingly, 360-degree feedback and competency modeling are closely aligned, especially in their application to training and development systems, as organizations seek to ensure they are focusing on the right competencies.

Four things are needed to implement a competency-based training and development system:

1. A set of behaviors that describe what the competencies look like on the job

2. A process to identify the extent to which people currently use the competencies

3. An awareness of training and development opportunities that help people learn and develop the competencies

4. A support and follow-up mechanism to ensure that skill and knowledge gaps are closed

Behavior Examples for Each Competency

Skills, knowledge, and characteristics can be abstract concepts that do not easily lend themselves to direct observation. Considered by name alone, competencies such as teamwork or self-sufficiency can be interpreted differently by different people. Only by observing behaviors that demonstrate the use of a competency can you decide if an individual possesses a skill, knowledge, or characteristic. Definitions of competencies must include behaviors that further define and clarify them so as to prevent misunderstanding them.

Let's use consulting as an illustration. One definition of that is checking with people before making decisions that affect them, encouraging participation in decision making, and allowing others to influence decisions. This is helpful but leaves room for interpretation and provides little guidance about behaviors required for effective consulting. It also makes it difficult to measure the frequency and effectiveness with which a person demonstrates the competency. Examples of good consulting behaviors could include the following:

- Asking people to help plan efforts or activities that require support and commitment
- Soliciting input on proposals
- Encouraging people to express concerns and doubts about your proposal
- Listening carefully to concerns or doubts about plans or strategies without getting defensive
- Modifying plans and strategies to deal with concerns and incorporate suggestions

How some sales competencies have been translated into behaviors is shown in Exhibit 6.5.

Identifying Strengths and Development Needs

Competency models show the behaviors most relevant to effective performance, and 360-degree feedback details behaviors needed on the job. Together, they help pinpoint areas that need to be developed to enhance job performance.

In recent years, 360-degree feedback has become popular as a way to learn about an individual's performance from bosses, direct reports, colleagues, and sometimes customers. Many think it provides a more comprehensive and accurate picture of behavior than traditional downward feedback from the boss and that it is, therefore, more useful in clarifying an individual's strengths and weaknesses.

Whether you use 360-degree feedback or the more traditional boss-coach/direct report method, the process should include two components: a means to collect data about use of competencies and a method for providing the person with results in a way that is easily understandable and action-oriented. Interviews or questionnaires can be used to collect data; the latter are used more frequently because they save time and money. A sample questionnaire based on behavior items from the sales competency model is shown in Exhibit 6.6.

Exhibit 6.5 Sales Competency Behavior Examples

Listening Beyond Product Needs

- Keeps customers regularly apprised of information and changes that might be important
- Suggests ways that customers can bring added value to their customers
- Shows customers to other suppliers and support services that can be of value
- Adds new dimensions to the customer relationship by creatively drawing on the full resources of the organization
- Gathers information to determine how customers value and use products

Establishing a Vision of a Committed Customer/Supplier Relationship

- Leads the process of articulating a clear and appealing framework of the customer/supplier relationship
- Creates a customer/supplier relationship that supports the mission, values, and aspirations of both organizations
- Develops customer/supplier relationships that are sensitive to the needs of other contributing functions in both organizations
- Communicates achievable objectives for the customer and supplier that also challenge the creativity of both
- Ensures that today's actions are linked to both organizations' strategic goals
- Ensures that the customer/supplier relationship is flexible and responsive to marketplace dynamics

Engaging in Self-Appraisal and Continuous Learning

- Demonstrates an understanding about what is working, what is not, and how things can be done differently
- Stays up to date in one's field of expertise
- Networks inside and outside of one's organization to broaden business knowledge and increase personal effectiveness
- Demonstrates continuous improvement in competence and skills
- Learns collaboratively with colleagues, not allowing competitiveness to get in the way
- Asks for and welcomes feedback to assess performances and the degree to which one is meeting expectations

Exhibit 6.6 Sales Competency 360-Degree Feedback Questionnaire

Please describe how often this manager uses each of the following specific behaviors. Read each statement carefully and mark your answer in the column to the right. For each of the practices, choose one of the following responses:

1. Never, not at all
2. Seldom, to a small extent
3. Sometimes, to a moderate extent
4. Usually, to a great extent
5. Almost always

The five numbered choices refer to how often this person uses this behavior. Please be as honest, objective, and accurate as possible.

Aligning Customer/Wholesaler Strategic Objectives

This person. . .

1. gathers information to understand customers' business strategies and their view of their market opportunities.	⑤ ④ ③ ② ①
2. keeps abreast of new developments and innovations in the customer's markets.	⑤ ④ ③ ② ①
3. keeps abreast of emerging trends and initiatives involving the industry's competitors.	⑤ ④ ③ ② ①
4. determines how his/her organization's strategic competencies help customers achieve strategic objectives.	⑤ ④ ③ ② ①
5. evaluates customer opportunities using a long-term perspective.	⑤ ④ ③ ② ①
6. welcomes opportunities to customize product/service offerings to assure they meet customers' long-term needs.	⑤ ④ ③ ② ①

Exhibit 6.6 Sales Competency 360-Degree Feedback Questionnaire, cont'd.

Utilizing Basic Selling Skills

This person. . . .

7. listens well to understand others' points of view. ⑤ ④ ③ ② ①
8. asks probing questions to help customers identify their needs. ⑤ ④ ③ ② ①
9. makes sure that his/her recommendations relate to customers' needs. ⑤ ④ ③ ② ①
10. asks for a decision when appropriate. ⑤ ④ ③ ② ①
11. moves forward in the sales process only when objections and concerns have been fully addressed. ⑤ ④ ③ ② ①
12. follows through on all elements of implementation once a recommendation is accepted. ⑤ ④ ③ ② ①

Building and Executing Strategic Account Penetration Plans

This person. . . .

13. positions him/herself with the "real" decision makers and influencers, and avoids getting sidetracked by those outside of the buying process. ⑤ ④ ③ ② ①
14. recognizes warning signs that indicate the customer relationship is in jeopardy. ⑤ ④ ③ ② ①
15. tracks account progress and asks for future business. ⑤ ④ ③ ② ①
16. focuses on both short-term and long-term account objectives. ⑤ ④ ③ ② ①
17. does appropriate "homework" prior to any customer contact. ⑤ ④ ③ ② ①
18. knows all the people, including end users, who are important to the successful purchase and ongoing use of his/her products and services. ⑤ ④ ③ ② ①

Feeding information back to people so that they understand it and do not become defensive is important if they are to use it to improve job performance. In our book, *The Art and Science of 360° Feedback* (Lepsinger and Lucia, 1997), we discuss the criteria for selecting an effective data collection method and the requirements of a high-quality feedback report. An example of a feedback report for the sales competency model is shown in Exhibit 6.7.

Awareness of Training and Development Opportunities

Addressing weaknesses in the feedback process requires knowing one's training and development options. These may include on-site training, university programs, and on-the-job experiences.

In the case of on-site training and university programs, a link between the program and the competency can be made quite clearly. Certain competencies—such as presentation skills, conflict management skills, or operating a machine—can be learned very well in a classroom.

Others, such as leadership and motivating people, are better learned in the real world. But it may be hard to find a link between this type of competency and a specific on-the-job experience—such as working on a task force or a cross-organizational project—that develops it. Seldom does any one job experience guarantee that a competency will be learned. Thus, clarifying which experiences are most appropriate for closing a skill gap or developing a competency can be challenging.

Fortunately, several training and development firms and academic institutions have begun to help. Three of these are the Center for Creative Leadership (see McCall, Lombardo, and Morrison, 1988), Personnel Decisions, Inc. (see Personnel Decisions International, 1996), and Lominger (see Lombardo and Eichinger, 1996). The texts referred to can help bosses, coaches, and human resource personnel select on-the-job experiences to develop the less tangible competencies.

Exhibit 6.7 Section of a Sales Competency Feedback Report

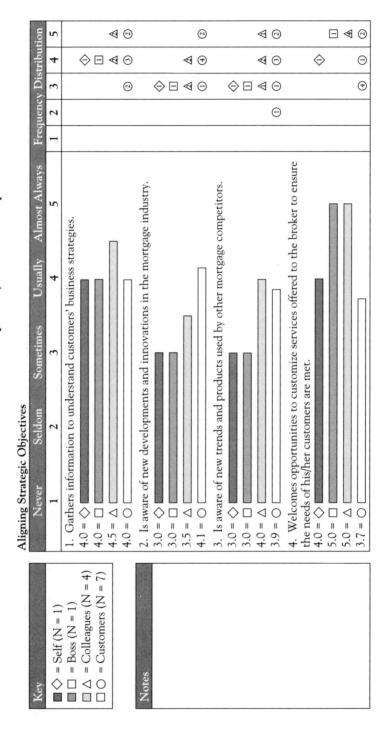

Aligning Strategic Objectives

Key
- ◇ = Self (N = 1)
- □ = Boss (N = 1)
- △ = Colleagues (N = 4)
- ○ = Customers (N = 7)

Rating scale: Never (1), Seldom (2), Sometimes (3), Usually (4), Almost Always (5)

1. Gathers information to understand customers' business strategies.
- 4.0 = ◇
- 4.0 = □
- 4.5 = △
- 4.0 = ○

2. Is aware of new developments and innovations in the mortgage industry.
- 3.0 = ◇
- 3.0 = □
- 3.5 = △
- 4.1 = ○

3. Is aware of new trends and products used by other mortgage competitors.
- 3.0 = ◇
- 3.0 = □
- 4.0 = △
- 3.9 = ○

4. Welcomes opportunities to customize services offered to the broker to ensure the needs of his/her customers are met.
- 4.0 = ◇
- 5.0 = □
- 5.0 = △
- 3.7 = ○

Notes

Support and Follow-Up

Experience has shown that ongoing support of training and development experiences helps make them stick. Without it, internalized learning that becomes a natural part of day-to-day behavior is less likely. Curricula should focus on the competencies that make the most difference in job performance. People can receive information on how well they currently exhibit a competency, attend training programs, or take a job assignment specifically to develop a competency, but without follow-up support they are likely to revert to their former behavior.

People learn best when they apply new information to real situations over time. Coaching discussions, training alumni to discuss progress and problems, development discussions with the boss, reinforcement of training concepts during team meetings, and the like help ensure that people take advantage of newly acquired competencies in their daily work.

Implementing a Competency-Based Appraisal System

Surprisingly, a competency-based appraisal system is no more difficult to implement than one that does not use competency models. All appraisal systems include guidelines by which capabilities should be reviewed and evaluated during the performance discussion. Unfortunately, the quality of these guidelines varies greatly. One client we worked with used only main headings such as leadership, management, and teamwork. Another wanted a flexible system that allowed the manager to focus on areas he or she felt were most relevant at the time. This system provided guidelines including, "What are this person's strengths? What has he/she done particularly well? What are this person's weaknesses? What does he/she need to do differently?" However, such vague or overly broad criteria can create problems during appraisal discussions: a lack of focus, difficulty arriving at agreement between the boss and direct report, or failure by the direct report to see the relevance of the criteria.

We believe that the key requirements for implementing a sound appraisal system are the same whether it is competency-based or not:

1. A description of relevant behaviors that everyone agrees is critical to job performance

2. A method to collect data on the behavior of the person being evaluated

3. The ability to have a constructive discussion

Competency-based appraisal increases the likelihood that appraisal discussions will be clear, address issues that directly relate to job performance, and achieve a balance between business objectives and how those objectives were achieved.

Description of Behaviors for Each Competency

A fault of many appraisal systems is their lack of sufficient information for appraisers to effectively and accurately monitor and evaluate performance. They tend to emphasize the measurement of *what* has been accomplished, with little attention to *how* it was accomplished. Competency-based appraisal addresses this by providing specific behavior examples against which to measure performance, ensuring that both the *what* and the *how* are evaluated.

There are two ways to illustrate behavior examples and incorporate them into an appraisal form. The first and most common is definitions of competencies that include observable characteristics. These make it clear what demonstrates the competencies. A rating scale is provided, from outstanding to unsatisfactory for example, to evaluate overall performance in the area of a given competency. See Exhibit 6.8 for an example.

The second form provides behavior examples that illustrate a range of effectiveness in demonstrating the competencies; Exhibit 6.9 is a sample. The advantage is that it provides concrete examples and reduces the subjectiveness of the evaluation. A disadvantage is that the examples tend to be generic and may still need to be interpreted to fit the particular situation.

Exhibit 6.8 Competencies with Definitions and Rating Scale

Rate the individual on each of the competencies using the 5-point rating scale.	*Rating scale:* Use this 5-point rating scale to indicate level of performance. (1) *Exceptional:* Consistently exceeds expectations (2) *Very good:* Consistently meets or exceeds expectations (3) *Good:* Consistently meets expectations (4) *Satisfactory:* Sometimes does not meet expectations (5) *Unsatisfactory:* Consistently fails to meet expectations

Competencies	Rating
Acts as a partner with the business units: Understands the internal and external issues facing the business unit clients and uses that understanding to forge partnerships and achieve goals	_____
Takes initiative: Proactively initiates changes or takes action to improve efficiency, address existing and potential problems, satisfy customers, and find new opportunities	_____
Gains support by influencing: Resolves disagreements, gains commitment to ideas, and ensures support for proposed actions and ideas	_____
Communicates effectively: Conveys information and ideas both orally and in writing and listens and responds appropriately to others	_____
Exhibits flexibility: Effectively adapts when faced with changing situations, unexpected pressures, and varying job demands	_____
Balances priorities: Manages workload effectively in light of multiple priorities	_____
Uses analytical skills: Uses relevant facts, data, and analytical tools to draw accurate and meaningful conclusions	_____

Exhibit 6.9 Competencies with a Range of Observable Behaviors from Above to Below Standard

Performance Review form

General Competencies

Points to consider. . .

- Ratings should be based on specific behaviors, not impressions
- Ratings should be based on day-to-day performance, not isolated incidents

Consider the definitions and place an x on the scale where it best reflects your direct report's behavior.

For the importance scale to the right, please circle how important you feel this behavior is to success in this person's position: H=High, M=Medium, L=Low.

Customer Focus		Importance: H M L
Strength	**Development Opportunity**	**Development Need**
Prioritizes internal and external customer needs; always uses knowledge of the customer to make decisions; gains customer's trust		Does not prioritize customer needs; seldom uses knowledge of the customer to make decisions; doesn't gain customer's trust

Comments

Ownership/Accountability
Importance: H   M   L

Development Opportunity

Development Need

Strength
Maintains motivation when faced with challenges; takes initiative beyond routine responsibilities; meets deadlines; owns mistakes

Loses motivation when faced with challenges; doesn't take initiative beyond routine work; misses deadlines; blames others when things go wrong

---

Informs/Clarifies
Importance: H   M   L

Development Opportunity

Development Need

Strength
Disseminates relevant information in a timely manner; provides clear direction; ensures objectives and priorities are understood

Slow to disseminate relevant information; provides little direction; rarely clarifies objectives, priorities, or deadlines

---

Provides Solution
Importance: H   M   L

Development Opportunity

Development Need

Strength
Anticipates problems and identifies their causes before implementing solutions; acknowledges when a plan is not working and takes appropriate steps to fix the problem

Seldom anticipates problems or identifies their causes before acting; doesn't act when it is clear a plan isn't working

Method for Data Collection

A competency model can help with data collection in two ways. First, it provides the manager with a specific list of behaviors to observe and monitor during the evaluation period. Second, if additional perspectives are sought, it enables the appraiser to conduct more focused, efficient conversations with the colleagues and customers of the person being reviewed.

As we have mentioned, the competency model can also be converted into a 360-degree questionnaire and used to collect relevant data from a large group of people in an efficient manner.

Ability to Have a Constructive Performance Discussion

Three factors are necessary to have a constructive performance discussion. First, the appraisal process itself must be perceived by the manager and the direct report as user-friendly rather than threatening or burdensome. A simple process contributes to both high levels of participation and better quality of results. Second, both parties need the communication and problem-solving skills to participate in a constructive discussion of strengths and development needs. Third, both parties need to come prepared for the discussion.

Simply implementing a competency-based system will not ensure that these criteria are met. However, when the competencies are perceived to be important and relevant to job performance, participation in the appraisal discussion tends to improve. A well-constructed model can help focus on the critical behaviors for successful performance. When this is the case, both the appraiser and the individual under review are more likely to take the discussion seriously and to devote time and energy to coming up with development plans and suggestions for improvement.

Implementing a Competency-Based
Succession Planning System

Four elements are required to implement an effective competency-based succession planning system:

1. Competency models for critical jobs and roles
2. A method to evaluate and develop succession candidates
3. An understanding of the methods and opportunities for developing competencies
4. The alignment of all human resource management systems

Competency Models for Key Jobs and Roles

Competency models have two applications in succession planning systems. First, they may be used as the basis for assessing and identifying high-potential employees. They allow you to look at the current pool of employees and determine who has the potential to fill key positions in the future. Second, the models help ensure that you are hiring people who have the potential to fill more senior positions in the company in the future.

For example, in our firm we have competency models for project coordinator and consultant positions. When we interview for a project coordinator, we base it on both competency models. The project coordinator model helps us assess if the person has the skills, knowledge, and characteristics to do that job. The consultant model enables us to determine if this person has the potential to do the consultant work should his or her interest lead in that direction. In fact, when we are hiring project coordinators, we are already looking at their potential to become consultants.

Monitor and Evaluate Candidate Performance

Although some succession planning systems keep the identity of high-potential managers a closely guarded company secret, we believe the best systems communicate to a candidate what he or she must do to be an effective contributor to the organization. These systems must also clarify what this means in terms of development (shared responsibility and personal commitment) and the individual's future career (no guarantee of promotion: career advances are earned based on performance and organizational needs).

Two forms for documenting the information required to adequately plan for a high-potential candidate's development, monitor progress, and evaluate readiness are shown in Exhibit 6.10. The first is an abbreviated form that shows a range of behaviors for each competency, from adequate to inadequate. This format, which is similar to the selection interviewing data form, can be used to focus discussions about a candidate's readiness in the most relevant job-related areas. Organizations might also consider additional assessment instruments (Spangenberg, 1990).

The second format, shown in Exhibit 6.11, is a bit more detailed. Instead of a range of behavior examples, this form uses a rating scale for each competency and includes a place to record development plans. Of course, components of each can be combined to create a single form that both evaluates readiness and records development plans for closing gaps or enhancing skills.

Methods and Opportunities to Develop the Competencies

Once a succession candidate's development gaps have been identified, the organization needs to invest the time and dollars to close them. It should determine which career opportunities should be made available to the candidate to enable him or her to gain the experience and knowledge required to fill more senior roles. Key players must be cooperative if development plans call for a candidate to move to a new assignment or take time away from the job for training. In theory, cooperation should be easier to obtain when everyone agrees that the development of these competencies is critical for success in the future role.

Alignment Among All Human Resource Management Systems

Succession planning is unique among human resource management processes in that it depends a great deal on the quality of input from other HRM systems. Because, as the saying goes, you can't make a silk purse out of a sow's ear, an organization must have a solid pool

Exhibit 6.10 Succession Planning Candidate Evaluation Form

Please evaluate the candidate using the 5-point scale and explanation of the rating in the space provided.

	Below Standard		Meets Standard		Above Standard
	1	2	3	4	5
Emotional Stamina	Ill at ease under pressure. Tense, nervous.		Satisfactory composure and effectiveness under pressure.		Entirely at ease. Relaxed, poised. Maintains effectiveness under pressure.
Why? _____					
Assertiveness	Submissive. Unable to assert self.		Assertive, moderately forceful.		Very assertive. Can readily take command of face-to-face situations.
Why? _____					
Self-sufficiency	Overly dependent. Difficulty functioning on own.		Adequately self-reliant.		Self-starting, proactive, independent.
Why? _____					
Sociability	Cold, aloof, unfriendly. Difficult to relate to.		Sufficiently amiable, friendly, and pleasant.		Exceptionally personable. Enjoys conversation and projects warmth.
Why? _____					

**Exhibit 6.11 Succession Planning
Candidate Evaluation and Development Planning Form**

			Rating				
Position	Possible Candidates	Ready When	Strategic Thinking	Managing Change	Developing People	Business Acumen	Next Steps

(1) = proven strength
(2) = meets expectations
(3) = needs improvement

of people to choose from. The best succession planning system in the world cannot succeed unless the selection, training and development, and appraisal systems all work effectively too. These systems must be designed to ensure that people who have the required capability or potential are hired, their ability is enhanced, and their potential is nurtured through learning experiences, coaching, and feedback. We strongly believe that the use of competency models across all human resource management systems will provide the necessary consistency and continuity.

Concluding Remarks

Much of the success of a competency model project hinges on translating the model into useable tools and formats for application in HRM systems. After all, the information gathered while developing the model will be of little value to people unless they have a means of applying it! And if they are not sure how to go about translating insight into action, the model is likely to sit on a shelf, and the time, money, and effort spent in developing it will be wasted. To avoid such an outcome, we offer the following suggestions to help you successfully integrate competency models into your HRM systems.

- Make sure that the purpose and importance of the competency model are understood by both the people who are responsible for using it in human resource practices and the individuals who will be measured against it. You may wish to hold training seminars or staff meetings to review the model's application in various HRM systems.

- The behavior examples included in the competency definition should be specific and applicable to the job or role under consideration. If an organization has identified customer focus as a core competency, behavior examples demonstrating it should be defined for each job or role. Remember, the behaviors a regional manager uses that demonstrate customer focus will be different from those of a sales associate.

- Solicit feedback about the usefulness of the model's application. Hold discussions with managers and incumbents to assess how well the model is being applied. For example, ask interviewers if the model is proving helpful during the selection process. Are hiring decisions based on the data resulting in improved performance? Do people feel that the model is helpful in pinpointing their development needs?

- Remember that the model is not set in stone. As the needs and landscape of a business shift, you will want to revisit the model to determine if it is still valid as a predictor of successful performance.

Now that you have an understanding of the development process and potential application of competency models, you are ready to sell the idea to others in your organization. In the final chapter, we discuss the process of creating support for the project among key decision makers and stakeholders.

Chapter Seven

Communicating Purpose and Gaining Commitment

Selling the Idea to Others in Your Organization

Even if you are convinced that using competency models can help your company achieve its strategic goals, you will probably have to convince others within the organization before embarking on a competency model project. Gaining the commitment of those with the authority to sign off on the decision—and those without formal authority whose ongoing good will and cooperation are nonetheless vital to the project's success—can be as important (and challenging!) a part of your task as developing the models themselves.

As any good salesperson knows, you usually get only one shot at making a pitch, so you'd better make sure it's good. In this chapter, we offer guidelines to help you develop a systematic plan to get support from those whose commitment is vital to success. First, however, let's assess your readiness to persuade others of the usefulness of competency models in your organization.

Becoming an Effective Advocate

You should ensure that you are well prepared to make a persuasive argument. To evaluate your readiness, ask yourself the following questions:

1. What specific business need do you hope to address through the use of a competency model, and what makes you believe that a competency model will be an effective tool for the purpose?

2. Do you feel ready to describe the process of developing a model, including the resources required to do so effectively

and the potential applications of the model? How do you propose to design the process to ensure its success?

3. Can you explain both the theoretical underpinnings of the process and how you intend to ensure that real, practical, long-term benefits will result?

If you are unable to answer any of these questions, you may wish to review the previous chapters before beginning the process of seeking support.

Once you have evaluated your own readiness and begun to prepare yourself, your next hurdle will be convincing others in your organization that developing a competency model is the action required, and that now is the time to act. In organizations where competency models have never been used before, or have been used with mixed or lackluster results, there may be resistance to the idea. But if you can show that it will directly address a business need and facilitate practical human resource decision making, people are more likely to listen.

Identifying Key Stakeholders and Expected Levels of Support

Before you can create an effective action plan for turning key individuals into champions, you have to decide exactly whose support will be vital and, based on your knowledge of them, anticipate their reactions to the proposal.

1. List All Stakeholders

This includes everyone who needs to be involved in the decision or who will be affected by it. List all the individuals and groups you can think of who might benefit, be negatively affected, or be inconvenienced. Don't forget, this might include members of your own team. Look for "hidden stakeholders," usually those who have personal reasons for not wanting a particular initiative to be implemented. (Such a reason might even include an unresolved conflict with one of those proposing the project.)

2. Categorize Your Stakeholders

To determine a stakeholder's likely level of support, you must first try to identify what each stands to gain or lose if your effort is successful.

Each stakeholder, whether an individual or a group, will view your effort from both an organizational and a personal perspective. To better anticipate reactions to your proposal, answer the following questions from each stakeholder's point of view: How will this project benefit my work unit (the part of the organization with which I identify most closely)? How might this project affect me personally?

Based on this analysis, try to categorize the stakeholders' expected level of support. Let's look at the varying degrees of support you can expect.

Commitment. Real commitment on the part of the decision maker or stakeholder will involve not only agreement that the competency model is needed, but also a willingness to proactively support the initiative. You will know that you have obtained the commitment you seek if the decision maker agrees to fund the effort, for example, or to use his or her group for a pilot, or to attempt to gain the support of other key stakeholders. If the decision maker offers to do such things before you have even asked, you know you really have an enthusiastic champion!

Compliance. Compliance is indicated by much more passive forms of agreement than those already indicated; often, it means that the person will do just what is asked or required, but no more. If, for example, the decision maker agrees not to block the effort, but will not try to gain the support of others, or if he or she agrees to allow some outstanding direct reports to be interviewed but will not be personally involved, you have not created a champion, although you have also not created an opponent. Of course, in some cases compliance is all that is required (for example, when a specific stakeholder is not needed to do anything to support the effort, but a general consensus among all stakeholders is desirable). However, if fuller participation is going to be needed at some point, or if the individual's lukewarm acceptance is a bar to gaining the commitment of others, you will probably want to try moving the person from compliance to genuine commitment.

Resistance. Active opposition to your request or plan—attempts to stop it from being implemented, to delay action on it, or a refusal to cooperate with requests pertaining to it (for example, not providing people for interviews or focus groups)—is, obviously, the reaction that will be most detrimental to the success of your proposal. Sometimes, in fact, silent resistance can be even worse than the open variety: someone may pretend to comply but will undermine the effort at every opportunity. The reason this is worse is that you may not be aware of the person's opposition until it has already caused damage.

As you probably realize, it is far easier to gain compliance than to secure enthusiastic commitment. However, for the competency model effort to be truly successful, full commitment will be needed from as many key people as possible. Otherwise they cannot possibly be effective advocates to others in the organization, nor will they give it their energetic support during the development and implementation phases.

3. Draw a Stakeholder Map

The easiest way to organize the information you collect about stakeholders is with a stakeholder map. You can create it alone, but you are less likely to omit anyone if you enlist colleagues who are also involved in the project. Use Exhibit 7.1 as a model. Put circles around stakeholders likely to support your effort, triangles around stakeholders who will comply but not actively support, squares around stakeholders likely to resist, and nothing around stakeholders you cannot categorize until you collect more information. Put the most important stakeholders—those with the most influence over your success or failure—close to the center of your map. Continue to collect the information you need to complete your map and update it as you learn more. You might also want to differentiate between those you need to involve from the outset and those you want to bring in at the data collection or validation stage. This decision should be based on what you want the stakeholder to do and what kind of authority or influence the individual has.

Exhibit 7.1 Sample Stakeholder Map

○ = Commitment

△ = Compliance

▭ = Resistance

☆ = Most Critical

Four Common Reasons for Lack of Commitment

Once you have identified key stakeholders and the degree of support you can expect from each, you need to focus your attention on those you believe will resist the idea of using competency models and those whose commitment is required but from whom you anticipate only compliance. Begin by trying to determine the likely reasons for their lack of commitment. Common reasons include the following:

1. The purpose of using a competency model is not made clear.
2. People are not involved in the development of the model.
3. People are concerned that they will be expected to behave differently toward their direct reports, bosses, or others.
4. Managers are afraid that using a competency model will limit their power of choice or require more work when they are hiring, developing, and evaluating people.

By identifying what concerns a person might have that could give rise to resistance, you can tailor your plan of approach to address these concerns directly.

Unclear Purpose for Using a Competency Model

When people lack a full understanding of how the competency model will be used, or of the business issue it will address, skepticism and suspicion greet your proposal. If the model is being developed for use in appraisal or compensation systems or a 360-degree feedback program, anxiety and rumors may also be rife.

Effective communication is the most powerful tool for eliminating this type of resistance and building support. Whether your competency model process is a major organizational intervention or a modest effort involving just a few people, frequent communication about it is important to its success. When one of our clients decided to develop competency models as the basis of a major training initiative, the CEO held a series of meetings with senior people across the organization to explain why it was important and what benefits were expected. In addition, people at all levels were kept aware of the project and informed of progress being made through e-mails, bulletin board notices, and items in the internal newsletter. The input of as many people as possible was solicited. Because of this high level of support and communication, the resistance that had been anticipated never really materialized.

Failure to Involve Enough Stakeholders

When stakeholders do not participate in the development stages of a project, they are much less likely to cooperate in its implementation. It is human nature for people to support what they help to create, but apart from ego gratification, their issues and needs must be fully addressed before they will devote time and effort to an initiative.

The most straightforward way to address this is to treat decision makers and other stakeholders exactly as you would external clients or customers. Take the time to understand their needs and involve them in the decision-making process. Involve as many stakeholders as possible in clarifying the business need, identifying or validating competencies, and designing project implementation. Throughout the process, solicit their ideas on how to overcome obstacles and win people over; sometimes, in the act of helping persuade others, they may be converted to real commitment themselves.

In our experience, a task force or temporary committee is particularly effective for ensuring the involvement of key individuals and building consensus. In the case of something like a major competency model project, it is more important to ensure that decisions are widely accepted than to make them quickly and unilaterally. Autocratic decision making is not likely to gain any champions for the project, so even if you feel that you are uniquely qualified to design the process it is wise to give others an equal say. As you must rely on many people to implement the decisions that are made, you want to be sure that they identify with decisions, understand the reasons for them, and therefore accept them wholeheartedly. Indeed, consultative decision making is often the best way to overcome resistance, because objections are likely to be raised in the course of group discussion and solutions can be arrived at that address them.

Concern About the Need to Behave Differently

Human beings may be inclined by nature to resist change. How much more resistant are they if they think that not just their environment but they themselves will have to change? Sometimes a competency model project is seen as a threat to the status quo and as an implied demand that people change their behavior. So supporting the initiative is seen as an implicit promise to do so.

One way to deal with this is to present the idea to people as an opportunity, which in fact it is. Because of its value as a clarifier, a competency model can help employees understand what is expected of them, what they can do to develop their strengths, and what elements of their jobs they should focus on to succeed. Rather than considering it a potential tool for negative judgment or a stick used to beat people into changing, they can be brought to see it as an aid to their own development and success. Furthermore, point out that a competency model will reinforce what people are doing right as well as what they need to do differently!

Fear of Limited Choices and Extra Work

A competency model may sound like a set of formulas for making what are, after all, highly complex and individual decisions. And as most people pride themselves on their instincts and abilities when it comes to human interactions, it's inevitable that they will resist the idea of having to follow preestablished, cut-and-dried criteria rather than their own skill and judgment. They will also fear losing the right to make their own choices and decisions: "I've always followed my gut instincts when hiring people, and now you're telling me I can only hire people who can juggle multiple priorities and are good at problem solving!?"

Point out that the competency model is not a matter of rigid formulas but of pointers—clues about what to look for, clarity about behaviors to nurture and encourage, assistance on how to determine development experiences that might help someone, and the like. For those concerned that their autonomy as managers—particularly as hirers, developers, and evaluators of others—will be threatened, the best response is to present the competency model as simply a tool to help them do their jobs even better, as well as a way of communicating to others what is important to the organization. So, far from being a substitute for individual judgment or decision making, it is an aid to it. Especially in situations where expectations of people are changing, you should also emphasize that a competency model allays a lot of fears and anxiety by articulating and clarifying the expectations to everybody concerned.

Prepare a Plan of Approach

We have found that having a specific action plan that includes exactly what you hope to achieve—what you want a particular person to do in support of the initiative—helps immeasurably when approaching key stakeholders. You can arrive at a comprehensive action plan by following these steps:

1. Name a decision maker or stakeholder.

2. Decide what you want that person to do—lend the use of a name, serve as a champion, provide funding? (Remember: decide when to approach a stakeholder based on when you want the person to take action.)

3. Identify the stakeholder's most important goals, values, and needs.

4. Clarify what the stakeholder would see as the benefits of the proposal. Identify both organizational and personal benefits.

5. Consider possible objections this person may raise during the discussion. How will you respond to each objection?

6. Determine the approach likely to work best with the stakeholder—fact based, value based, or collaborative.

7. Decide how you will begin the conversation. What will your opening remarks be?

8. Think about what factors (a history of friendly relations, a shared belief in the need to address the business issue) will make the conversation easy. What can you do to leverage these factors?

9. Think about what factors (a past negative experience with a human resource initiative, skepticism about the diversion of resources from other tasks at hand) will make the conversation difficult. What can you do or say to lessen the difficulty?

Common Objections to Competency Models

Here we examine the most frequently raised objections to the use of competency models and offer appropriate rebuttals that we hope will help in your conversations with stakeholders.

Too Time-Consuming and Too Costly

We were recently called in to confer with a senior human resources executive of a financial services company that was undergoing a culture change requiring a much greater degree of autonomy and individual decision making from its employees. The CEO had given him the task of investigating competency model options as a way of identifying future job requirements, the gaps between future needs and current skills, and the training requirements suggested by those gaps. A feedback process based on the competency models was also a possibility.

The HR manager described what the company had in mind and asked for a rough estimate of the people, dollars, and time that would be required to implement the development process, the integration of the models into the company's various HR systems, and the 360-degree feedback program. As we proceeded to do so, he began tapping his pencil on the desk and staring out the window. Finally, he interrupted to say, "Let me be honest with you. I just don't think that senior management is ready to make anything like the sort of commitment you're describing. I think I'd better go back to them and talk it over before taking up any more of your time." The last we heard, the project had been put on hold indefinitely.

Every year, various departments, functions, and businesses within an organization engage in an inevitable tug-of-war over how resources are going to be allocated—who gets what when. Each program must be justified in terms of productivity and dollars, and those that reap easily quantifiable results may be favored. In the case of competency models, it may not be easy to point to direct financial savings, as may be possible with, for example, technology upgrades or the elimination of certain jobs. The time, people, and money you are asking for may seem excessive to those skeptical about HR initiatives that net only "fuzzy" results.

Your response to this objection should be couched in terms of the specific business need you will address through competency models and the specific benefits that will result. For example, if a training need is being addressed, the expected benefit you want to cite might relate to increased productivity: people trained in the skills they really need will perform better.

When appropriate, cite other organizations that have successfully addressed similar issues by using competency models. For example, if a business need is to improve the selection of new salespeople so that turnover rates go down, talk about the current cost of recruiting, hiring, and training, the high turnover rate, and how determining what sort of applicants to look for during selection has helped other organizations reduce their attrition rate for salespeople.

Finally, be prepared to discuss alternative approaches to the problem and to explain, if necessary, why you think developing a competency model would be the most effective way to go.

How Can Any One Model Work for Everyone?

This objection is based on a misunderstanding of competency models. The belief that they define the necessary skills for performing all roles and jobs leads to the suspicion that crucial distinctions are missing and that the model must be so vague and general as to be totally useless. But actually, even when a model is couched in terms of core competencies such as adding value for customers, the behaviors being measured vary a great deal depending on role.

You can counter this objection by explaining that the competency model will be delineated in behavioral terms, and that the behaviors measured will differ depending on the job or role. The goal is to provide an agreed-upon definition of how the varying competencies for each targeted job or role can be demonstrated. Showing actual examples of competency models can also help to overcome suspicions.

Too Much Change Is Required; Too Many People Will Feel Let Down

When the proposal calls for the competency model to revamp the human resource systems, or is the basis for 360-degree feedback, some managers may be afraid that radical change will be expected of them. This may give them cold feet. Some may also worry that if people are told that the new models will be used to develop new systems or bring about real culture change, too much will be expected: "We will just be setting people up for another anticlimax, another disappointment." Such concerns are particularly common when the competency model is to be used for 360-degree feedback or appraisal; people fear that getting or giving negative feedback could play havoc with on-the-job relationships and interfere with getting work accomplished.

Your response to this should focus on the link between the behaviors being measured and the organization's readiness to meet future challenges. Argue that the real risk lies not in creating inflated expectations—which can largely be avoided anyway by properly presenting the project to employees and by giving them time to make the transition to new behaviors—but in missing the opportunity to bring about needed changes. If the behaviors crucial to success are not practiced widely enough, any effort to bring them into focus and ensure that people work to develop the skills they need is less risky than burying the organization's collective head in the sand. Senior managers are more likely to support competency-based HRM systems if they think the organization's future could be at stake.

A Competency Model Simply Isn't Necessary

The assumption underlying this objection is that most employees already know what they and others need to do to be effective: People either get it or they don't, so why spend a lot to prove scientifically what everyone already understands at gut level? Shouldn't employees instead attend to their work and not be distracted by competency projects?

As one senior manager put it when we were discussing developing a competency model for his organization, "I could call in any one of my best people and get them to tell you what it takes to get things accomplished around here. Do we have to get so academic about it?" In the end, he rejected the proposal because he distrusted the idea that any outsider could come in and tell his employees what they need to do to succeed.

To respond to such notions, make the point that competency models ask people within the organization precisely what is required to help the organization succeed: their input determines which behaviors are emphasized and which are not. You might add that if you ask six people what makes someone effective, you quite likely will get six slightly different answers. Developing a competency model takes those six answers and focuses on the points where they overlap! It therefore helps clarify people's shared beliefs about what it means to be a good manager in a manner that is unbiased rather than based on individual (often biased) opinions. The final outcome may indeed validate gut feelings, but the very process ensures that assessment relates to established performance criteria.

This type of objection, which is often rooted in skepticism about HR initiatives in general, can also be countered by citing other companies in the same or similar industries that used a competency model and achieved good business results. (Some of the case studies in Chapter Two might be relevant.) Also, point out that the competitive environment is changing, which means the organization needs to change too; part of the practical value of a competency model lies in its ability to test assumptions about what it takes to succeed. It may be worthwhile to see if traditional beliefs hold true in the current environment.

Why Spend Time on the Competencies du Jour?

One argument for using competency models is that they prepare organizations for change and can help bring it about. So it might seem that an argument against them is that things are bound to change yet again: Why bother to adapt to Change A when it won't help us with Change B? Why not just ride things out as best we can?

The answer is that fundamental shifts in what an organization needs to do to compete—such as responding more quickly to market needs or altering the pattern of decision making—are not likely to go away soon. Specific, one-time change is not the concern of competency models, but rather the fundamental, deep-rooted change in global markets and in corporate culture.

For example, one major change faced in the past decade was a shift to more horizontal structures of management; more and more people have to be decision makers, more and more people have to work together as equals on teams and committees rather than in traditional boss-subordinate relationships. Increased focus on the customer, the need for employees to be accountable for entire work processes rather than just their individual functions, and the pressure for autonomy brought about by downsizing all make it unlikely that the trend away from vertical relationships is going to change soon. So whatever may change in the future, traditional relationships are unlikely to return.

Moreover, competency models seek to identify the competencies needed to succeed in any environment, good and bad times alike. The ability to inspire or influence people over whom one has no direct authority is a competency that can take many forms in different situations, but is consistently likely to contribute to success.

People Won't Agree on One Model; The Organization Is Too Diverse

Certainly, diversity is strength—and of course different jobs demand different skills and knowledge. An R&D scientist and a training professional, or a sales representative and an operations manager, are likely to have very different skills and make very different contributions. The same may also hold true for someone in the field versus someone at headquarters. The competency model may be seen as an attempt to fit all these unique individuals into a common mold.

But this is a failure to see the forest for the trees. If we concentrate only on the difference between roles, we lose sight of commonalities that are the basis for organizational success. Big-picture thinking, which focuses on underlying links rather than specific differences, is helpful precisely because it clarifies traits and behaviors that are just as essential for the R&D scientist as for the sales representative. Similarly, competency models help to clarify culture and values. Unconsciously, we may be aware of some of this; for example, we may know that being able and willing to apply oneself to a task or to process information are generic competencies that everyone needs. And it is likely that people at headquarters have some of the same competencies as those in the field.

Effective competency models take into account not only the essential similarities but the differences in what is required to play different roles. Thus, you can respond to this objection by pointing out the value of clarifying fundamental similarities and explaining the ways that competency models are tailored to differing roles.

Competency Models Are for Hourly Workers, Not Leaders

The idea that managerial and leadership skills can be measured and quantified is troubling to some. They may point out that identifying the skills to succeed on an assembly line is one thing and determining the complex and subtle abilities needed to lead many people is quite another.

Generally, this objection is raised by people who have never seen a competency model or don't understand them. Probably the best thing you can do is show them one for an actual leadership role and describe various organizations where competency models have been used with senior-level managers. Also, explain just how the proposed competency model will be used and exactly why you feel it is the best way to address the business issue involved.

Exhibit 7.2 summarizes the various causes of resistance or lack of commitment and recommends actions to address each one.

Concluding Remarks

As you embark on your campaign to gain the support of key stakeholders, you are more likely to achieve your goal if you follow these guidelines:

1. Use your past experiences with the stakeholder to identify the approach that is likely to be most effective.
2. Anticipate objections and be prepared to address any questions or concerns.
3. Listen carefully. Show you are listening by paraphrasing what has been said, then directly address the stakeholder's issues or concerns.
4. Be flexible. Be willing to address problems and incorporate others' suggestions and concerns into your planning.

Finally, remember always to focus on the relationship between the model and the achievement of organizational goals!

Exhibit 7.2 Causes of Resistance
and Recommended Actions to Address Each

Resistance Source	Recommended Actions
Purpose of competency model initiative not made clear	Hold an informal discussion with individuals or teams to review reasons for development and implementation of the model and to answer any questions
	Circulate a memo including rationale and details on how you will proceed
	State explicitly what new behaviors are needed and why
	Hold a series of town meetings to review the business need the competency model initiative will address
Do not see need for introducing competency models into current human resource systems	Explain one on one what the model will do to make the current system(s) easier to use
	Describe what is inadequate about the current system(s) and how the model will make the system(s) more effective
Not involved in planning the development of the competency model	Invite small groups to be advisors during the planning process
	Review action plans with individuals who have concerns about timing and solicit ideas on how to adjust or fine-tune the plan
	Use key stakeholders to identify potential problems and ask them to generate ideas to avoid the problems
	Be flexible regarding deadlines, taking into account critical internal activities such as product introductions, year-end reviews, and the like
Cost too high or reward is inadequate for supporting the effort	Speak in the "language of management" regarding cost/benefit, that is, how cost of turnover can be reduced, how training dollars can be better focused, and how recruiting cycle can be shortened

Exhibit 7.2 Causes of Resistance
and Recommended Actions to Address Each, cont'd.

Resistance Source	Recommended Actions
	Review the actions for developing the model—ideally, where the cost of external resources might be reduced by getting greater participation by internal resources
	Consider using pilots to show the value of the process on a smaller scale before investing in a large-scale project
Doubt organizational resources/ follow-through to actually finish the development or implementation	Demonstrate visible support by senior management in a meeting, memos, and the like; demonstrate resources committed
	Change reward systems (monetary and/or nonmonetary) to encourage the use of the model
	Use stakeholders to help identify what is necessary to ensure support later
	Provide prototypes on how the end product will actually be applied to human resource systems (show that you've thought through the issues)
Implementation of model occurs too quickly/slowly	Be on the lookout for signs that the process is losing momentum—call on high-level supporters to show their commitment
	Ensure sufficient resources to get the job done
	Plan small steps and quick successes to win over skeptics—keep the process simple
	Provide accomplishments to date that show progress
	Pace the implementation so as not to over-whelm people—be sensitive to the other demands of their jobs
History of poorly implemented changes to human resource systems/processes	If true, make clear why and how this one will be different

Exhibit 7.2 Causes of Resistance
and Recommended Actions to Address Each, cont'd.

Resistance Source	Recommended Actions
	Do a postmortem with skeptics on why the last one(s) failed—what will it take to avoid the same problems? What worked?
	Speak with people in the organization who have implemented major changes successfully (for example, new technology, new product development process, and the like) and get advice on how to ensure success
Concern about what "using it" really means	Provide training and guidance on the use and implementation of the model
	Make the related tools easy to use with straightforward, stand-alone instructions
	Set up hot lines to provide tips on the tools
	Tailor the tools to the needs of functions or businesses so there will be instant credibility

Resource A:
Validated Generic
Competency Models

This resource contains examples of two competency models—one for leadership and management and one for sales. They were developed for specific roles (leader or salesperson) and describe the competencies required for success. Our research indicates that, in general, people who frequently use these competencies tend to have more effective work units and are perceived to be more effective on the job than those who use them less frequently.

Leadership and Managerial Practices

Informing: Disseminating relevant information about decisions, plans, and activities to people who need the information to do their work

Clarifying: Assigning work, providing direction on how to do the work, and communicating a clear understanding of job responsibilities, task objectives, priorities, deadlines, and performance expectations

Monitoring: Gathering information about work activities and external conditions affecting the work, checking on the progress and quality of the work, and evaluating the performance of individuals and the effectiveness of the organizational unit

Planning: Determining long-term objectives and strategies, allocating resources according to priorities, determining how to use personnel and resources efficiently to accomplish a task or project, and determining how to improve coordination, productivity, and effectiveness

Problem solving: Identifying work-related problems, analyzing problems in a systematic but timely manner, and acting decisively to implement solutions and resolve crises

Consulting: Checking with people before making changes that affect them, encouraging participation in decision making, and allowing others to influence decisions

Delegating: Assigning responsibilities to direct reports and giving them discretion and authority to carry them out

Influencing: Using influence techniques that appeal to reason, values, or emotion to generate enthusiasm for the work, commitment to task objectives, or compliance with orders and requests

Recognizing: Giving praise and showing appreciation to others for effective performance, significant achievements, and special contributions

Rewarding: Providing tangible rewards such as a pay increase or promotion for effective performance and demonstrated competence

Supporting: Acting friendly and considerate, being patient and helpful, and showing sympathy and support when someone is upset and anxious

Mentoring: Providing career counseling and facilitating someone's skill development and career advancement

Networking: Socializing informally, developing contacts with people who are a source of information and support, and maintaining contacts through periodic visits, telephone calls, correspondence, and attendance at meetings and social events

Team building: Facilitating the constructive resolution of conflict, and encouraging cooperation, teamwork, and identification with the organizational unit

Sales Competency Model

Aligning customer-supplier strategic objectives: identifying new opportunities and applications that add value for customers and enhance the value of the relationship for the salesperson's organization

Listening beyond product needs: seeing business process improvement potential and opportunities to add value to the salesperson's customers.

Understanding the financial impact of decisions: on both customers and on the salesperson's organization, and quantifying and communicating the value of the relationship

Orchestrating organizational resources: identifying key contributors, communicating relevant information, and building collaborative, customer-focused relationships

Using consultative problem solving: creating new solutions, customized products and services, and paradigm changes while being willing and able to work outside the norm when necessary

Establishing a vision of a committed customer-supplier relationship: supporting the mission, values, and aspirations of both organizations

Engaging in self-appraisal and continuous learning: securing feedback from customers, colleagues, and managers

Utilizing basic selling skills: establishing rapport, uncovering needs, relating benefits to product features, handling objections, and closing

Building and executing strategic account penetration plans: mapping the process for doing business with customers

See Rothwell (1996) for a description of core competencies of Human Performance Enhancement Specialists, and Rothwell, Prescott, and Taylor (1998) for a description of Human Resource Management Leadership Competencies.

Resource B: Position-Specific Competency Models

The competency models in this resource were developed for specific jobs in specific companies. In each case we validated the model to ensure that we had identified the competencies that differentiated the most successful incumbents from those who are less successful. Most of these models were developed from scratch, although the sales consultant model is based on our generic sales competency model.

Competency Definitions for Finance Employees

Acts as a partner with the business units: Understands the internal and external issues facing business unit clients and uses that understanding to forge partnerships and achieve goals

Builds relationships: Achieves mutual objectives by informing and involving others in solving problems and implementing changes

Takes initiative: Proactively initiates changes or takes action to improve efficiency, address existing and potential problems, satisfy customers, and find new opportunities

Gains support by influencing: Resolves disagreements, gains commitment to ideas, and ensures support for proposed actions and ideas

Communicates effectively: Conveys information and ideas both orally and in writing and listens and responds appropriately to others

Exhibits flexibility: Effectively adapts when faced with changing situations, unexpected pressures, and varying job demands

Balances priorities: Manages workload effectively in light of multiple priorities

Applies knowledge of financial systems: Leverages a thorough knowledge of financial systems throughout the organization to fulfill responsibilities

Uses analytical skills: Uses relevant facts, data, and analytical tools to draw accurate and meaningful conclusions

Uses a computer effectively: Uses computer systems and software to gather and analyze data, communicate with others, and improve efficiency

Competency Definitions
for a Branch Technical Liaison

Technical Knowledge

Computer literacy: Basic knowledge of the main elements of a computer, computer peripherals, networks, and DOS and Windows operating systems

Familiarity with off-the-shelf software: Broad understanding of the most common off-the-shelf programs used at the firm and the ability to teach users how to get the maximum value out of their software by showing them new functions, teaching them how to avoid problems, or creating custom configurations that improve productivity; additionally, serving as resource for frequently asked questions and solving common problems

Knowledge of the firm's unique software and hardware systems: Clear understanding of hardware and software systems unique to the firm and the potential problems or conflicts associated with them; also, knowing which branch personnel use which parts of the system and their objectives in doing so

Knowledge of the firm's trading systems: Understanding how trading systems work and how they are used by brokers, sales assistants, and other personnel; knowing the firm's markets and the securities industry

Planning and Organizing

Prioritization/time management: Allocating time among various responsibilities and prioritizing issues quickly and appropriately to ensure that the branch's needs are met; establishing and maintaining systems that ensure the completion of routine tasks, updates, and training; ability to reprioritize daily tasks to resolve urgent issues that arise without losing sight of longer-term projects

Ability to handle multiple tasks: Ability to maintain focus on a task or project in the face of numerous incoming telephone calls, questions, and requests; when interrupted, ability to judge whether to pursue the new issue or continue working on the earlier one; ability to shift attention quickly to respond to the unexpected while progressing on others that range from the mundane to the critical

Persistence/follow-through: Ability to see issues through to complete resolution, checking with the branch, home office, other personnel, or outside vendors until they know that the issue or problem has been completely resolved; ability to overcome systems or structural barriers that initially prevent resolution of problems

Solution Orientation

Problem solving: Ability to take great pride and satisfaction in helping others solve problems by determining the nature of a problem by asking appropriate questions and reviewing documentation, determining probable causes, and taking appropriate measures to resolve the issue in a timely manner; these might involve communicating with Technology Services or obtaining additional information from users or outside vendors. Also, the ability to establish systems and procedures to ensure that a problem will not recur in the future

Adaptability/flexibility: Ability to rearrange schedules (work and personal) to meet the needs of the business and respond quickly to situations created by changes or unanticipated problems; ability to adapt to the different working styles and knowledge levels of the people they support

Communication Skills

Oral communication: Ability to speak with clients, brokers, and other staff members clearly, professionally, and tactfully; ability to explain complicated issues and procedures simply and accurately; ability to discern a user's level of computer knowledge and provide information in a way the user will understand; ability to translate highly technical language into terms easily understood by end users

Listening: Ability to pick out important information in oral communications, clearly understand complex instructions, and ask appropriate questions to clarify issues and problems; being able to demonstrate hearing others' concerns, to understand the problem, and to be both willing and able to take appropriate next steps

Maintaining open relationships: Maintaining clear lines of communication with a wide range of individuals based on a high degree of trust and credibility; encouraging people to approach them with problems or mistakes and try to involve them in the solutions; being able to help others improve their computing skills

Relationship Skills

Empathy: Understanding the pressures facing brokers, operations personnel, sales assistants, and branch managers and respond appropriately; displaying sensitivity to the needs and concerns of others and ability to communicate with them tactfully even in high-pressure situations or when they are clearly upset; enjoyment in dealing with people and ability to work with people of diverse styles and backgrounds

Influencing: Ability to persuasively present ideas to gain commitment from others, win concessions without damaging relationships, and influence, motivate, and persuade others to change their priorities, including operations personnel, brokers, sales assistants, branch managers, help-desk staffers, and other related personnel; ability to establish procedures and practices that the branch must follow, to convey them clearly, and to build acceptable support for them

Personal Qualities

Endurance: Capacity and willingness to complete work that is unchallenging or mundane, capability of working long and unpredictable hours without a break, and ability to maintain an appropriate pace and tempo when handling multiple tasks and deadlines

Initiative/self-reliance: Ability to work with minimum direction, support, or approval and maintain motivation even when the office environment is not upbeat; ability to constantly look for better ways to organize their work and time and serve the branch by proactively seeking ways to improve technology systems and end users' understanding of them; refusing to settle for unsatisfactory or incomplete answers and aggressively seeking information they need even when it is not readily available

Stress tolerance: Ability to handle work pressures, the uncertainty and variability of the securities industry, and complex computer systems while maintaining poise and an even temper; ability to thrive on variety and deal with unexpected problems, even when these disrupt planned activities; ability to stay effective in extremely high-pressure situations in order to troubleshoot technological problems that can cripple a branch

Continuous learning: Willing to seek opportunities for continuous learning; able to treat the unexpected as a chance to learn something new; thriving on the opportunity to explore new areas and delighting in acquiring new knowledge not just because it improves their effectiveness but for the sheer pleasure of learning more about computers, the company, and the securities industry

Training Skills

Training: Ability to help new users learn the basics of the systems they use, ensure that all users have a standard level of computer literacy, and show users how to use appropriate guides, manuals, and supporting documentation; ability to explain complex and possibly intimidating processes to people who may be unfamiliar with computers and, in larger branches, to run training classes that help end users learn new functions of both standard software and company systems

Coaching: Ability to help others by proactively identifying opportunities for users to enhance productivity through technology and showing them how to perform tasks more efficiently and effectively; ability to work with end users to help them understand systems they work with so that they can avoid or solve problems; ability to develop assistant BTLs by teaching them basic BTL functions such as tape backups and troubleshooting

Disseminating information: Remaining current on all system and software changes and updates and actively seeking information that might be needed to prepare for upcoming changes; keeping all members of their branch, including brokers, sales assistants, branch managers, and operations managers, clearly informed about upcoming changes and how they are likely to have an impact on the branch

Competency Definitions for a New Associate in a Law Firm

Abilities

Writing skills: Ability to draft agreements, letters of intent, term sheets, SEC filings, briefs, and correspondence, as well as to put issues into words quickly and to express ideas clearly and concisely on paper

Oral communication skills: Ability to interview witnesses and clients, conduct telephone communications, negotiate contracts and terms of settlement, engage in face-to-face client contact, get information, give information, and condense and communicate complex topics clearly and concisely, including using gestures and other non-verbal communication

Detail handling: Ability to review details of documents quickly, keep accurate diaries, and produce error-free work, including accurate citations, grammar, figures, and the like

Critical, analytical, and logical thinking: Ability to understand implications of rulings (recent and past), critically review documents, think inductively and deductively, draw conclusions from limited or related information, seek relevant information, determine the source of a problem, identify relationships, and respond to the subtleties of problem solving

Planning and organizing: Ability to organize and prioritize the workload while maintaining focus and staying on track, establish and implement an efficient course of action, understand what's necessary to get things done, use resources optimally, balance the workload when involved in multiple projects or cases, and establish appropriate deadlines

Mental agility: Ability to become quickly oriented to assignments, shift gears and change direction when necessary, innovate and divergently approach problems, quickly understand and respond, pursue related information, understand relation of work to mission and purposes of assignment, answer questions posed and probe for further questions, raise additional relevant issues, identify connections between issues, identify impact of changes, and go beyond the obvious

Relationship Skills

Tactfulness: Ability to "wear well" with partners, clients, and peers in one-on-one consultations and in group meetings; display poise and diplomacy; tactfully respond to partners' requests; avoid abrasiveness when negotiating; and maintain communication in adversarial situations

Understanding people: Perceiving and responding to behavioral cues; having insight into the reasons underlying the behavior and actions of others; and being able to analyze the motives and feelings of colleagues, clients, outside counsel, and others

Influencing/negotiating: Ability to influence others within and outside the company; persuasively present thoughts and ideas; negotiate in difficult situations; make appropriate trade-offs; win concessions without damaging relationships; and influence, motivate, and persuade others in order to achieve company and client objectives

Managing people: Ability to identify appropriate resources for a variety of assignments, clearly explain assignments, provide useful feedback on work and behavior, motivate people, delegate, and build teams

Listening skills: Ability to discern and respond to the feelings and underlying messages of clients, colleagues, and others; pick out important information in oral communications; pay attention to orally presented facts and details; and appreciate feelings and concerns heard in conversation

Personal Qualities

Achievement motivation: Having a desire for increased responsibility, seeing things through to completion, being tenacious, having an intrinsic need to do things well, accumulating a repertoire of accomplishments, enthusiastically doing what is necessary to get the job done, and striving to meet standards and expectations of partners and clients

Competitiveness: Desire to succeed at negotiation, win for our clients, and meet or exceed expectations

Initiative/self-reliance: Ability to anticipate client and partner needs; work with a minimum of direction, support, or approval; be active in influencing events (seeking out challenging work); be a self-starter; and maintain motivation for a long time

Adaptability/flexibility: Ability to rearrange schedule (work and life) quickly, work with open-ended time frames (closing meetings, trials), respond to the unpredictable mentally and physically, and tolerate long time horizons

Stress tolerance: Ability to handle work pressures while maintaining effectiveness, draft under time pressure, meet multiple short-term deadlines, and handle multiple top priorities

Self-confidence: Is self-assured, inspires confidence in the firm, displays project expertise on subject matter, is willing to challenge others' thinking with assertiveness and clarity (including that of partners), performs effectively in front of those with greater experience and knowledge, deals with criticism, and commands attention and maintains control in an adversarial setting

Endurance: Has the capacity and willingness to see projects through in every detail; is persistent, tenacious, and detailed even when doing work that is unchallenging or mundane; can work long hours and days without a break, juggle many projects at once, and maintain appropriate pace and tempo when handling multiple tasks and deadlines

Reflectiveness/introspection: Willing to admit mistakes and not blame others, learn from mistakes, understand limitations and use them as an opportunity for growth, review projects objectively, avoid defensiveness, and handle criticism constructively

Competency Definitions for a Research Associate in a Consulting Firm

Technical Activities

Quantitative reasoning: Ability to analyze, interpret, and understand data sensibly, draw conclusions from limited or ambiguous data, and explain quantitative findings to clients and consultants

Attention to detail: Ability to process, code, and double-check data completely and accurately; proofread tables, charts, and text; review details of documents in short time periods; double-check type-setting and duplication; and produce error-free work

Computer literacy: Must feel comfortable with computers and technology, derive satisfaction from working with computers, and have a basic aptitude for computers that will enable learning the software used at our firm for data analysis

Endurance: Has the capacity and willingness to see projects through in every detail; be persistent, tenacious, and detailed even when doing work that is unchallenging or mundane; be capable of working long hours and days without a break, juggle many projects, and maintain appropriate pace and tempo when handling multiple tasks and deadlines

Program Coordination

Prioritizing and organizing: Ability to organize and prioritize work while maintaining focus and staying on track, establish and implement an efficient course of action, understand what's necessary to get things done, use resources optimally, balance the workload when involved in multiple projects, and establish appropriate deadlines

Achievement motivation: Have an intrinsic need to succeed and excel, see things through to completion, be tenacious, accumulate a repertoire of accomplishments, enthusiastically do what is necessary to get the job done, and strive to meet standards and expectations of consultants and clients

Initiative/self-reliance: Ability to anticipate client and consultant needs, work with a minimum of direction and support, maintain self-confidence and self-esteem even without others' explicit approval, and maintain motivation over extended periods

Adaptability/flexibility: Ability to rearrange one's schedule (work and life) quickly and be responsive to pressing, unexpected requests from consultants and clients

Critical, analytical thinking: Possesses inductive and deductive thinking ability, can draw conclusions from limited or related information, proactively seeks relevant information, determines the source of a problem, identifies relationships, and can respond to the subtleties of problem solving

Mental agility: Ability to quickly orient to assignments, shift gears and change direction when working on multiple projects in different stages of the program cycle, innovate and creatively approach problems, quickly understand and respond, pursue related information, intelligently answer questions posed by consultants and clients and probe for further questions, identify connections between issues, and go beyond the obvious

Stress tolerance: Ability to handle work pressures and tolerate brusque treatment while maintaining effectiveness, work under time pressure, meet multiple short-term deadlines, and handle multiple top priorities

Self-confidence: Be self-assured and able to handle criticism, display project expertise on subject matter, be willing to challenge others' thinking with assertiveness and clarity, be able to perform effectively in front of those with greater experience and knowledge, and have the confidence to ask questions and be proactive

Relationship Management

Oral communication skills: Ability to engage in face-to-face and telephone contact with clients and consultants, get information, give information, condense and communicate complex topics clearly and concisely, and defend ideas to others

Tactfulness: Ability to "wear well" with consultants, clients, and peers in face-to-face and telephone contact, display poise and diplomacy, tactfully respond to consultants' requests, avoid abrasiveness when negotiating, and maintain communication in adversarial situations

Managing people: Ability to identify appropriate resources for a variety of assignments, clearly explain assignments, motivate people, delegate, build teams, and interact with people at different levels

Understanding of people: Can perceive and respond to behavioral cues, has insight into the reasons underlying the behavior and actions of others, and is able to analyze and empathize with the motives and feelings of others at all levels (clients, consultants, peers, administrative staff, vendors, and others).

Influencing/negotiating: Ability to influence others in the firm; persuasively present thoughts and ideas; negotiate in difficult situations; make appropriate trade-offs; win concessions without damaging relationships; negotiate work completion dates; and influence, motivate, and persuade others in order to meet pressing deadlines

Listening skills: Ability to discern and respond to the feelings and underlying messages of clients, colleagues, consultants, and others; pick out important information in oral communications; pay attention to orally presented facts and details; and appreciate feelings and concerns heard in conversation

Reflectiveness/introspection: Willingness to admit mistakes and not blame others, learn from mistakes, understand limitations and use them as an opportunity for growth, use consultant feedback for self-improvement, review projects objectively, avoid defensiveness, and handle criticism constructively

Sociability: Ability to relate to peers and enjoy working on a team, partaking in social activities with coworkers, and being part of an informal social support network in the office

Nurturing/patience: Ability, when in a mentoring role, to patiently serve as a mentor and further the development of new research assistants, teach and thoroughly explain the responsibilities of the job to them, and provide them with social support as well as professional guidance

Competency Definitions for an
Automobile Sales Consultant

Skills

Communication skills: Ability to be understood and to understand the customer; use questioning and active listening; provide information useful to the customer; ability to make customers feel comfortable by greeting them, making eye contact, and acting in a friendly manner

Basic selling skills: Ability to establish rapport with the customer, listen effectively to identify customer needs, and relate the benefits of product features; handle objections and close the sale

Organizational skills: Ability to keep accurate customer records, conduct periodic follow-ups with customers before and after the sale, track personal progress toward sales targets and goals, pay attention to details, and manage time effectively

Customer focus: Ability to operate with the customer's best interest in mind, position for repeat business by delighting and surprising the customer, make the customer feel important, and strive for customer satisfaction throughout the entire sales and delivery process

Conflict management: Ability to resolve differences with customers and colleagues and reach agreement by maintaining a problem-solving attitude

Knowledge

Product knowledge: Having a basic understanding of products and services, including features, benefits, and relevant performance statistics; keeping up to date with the latest information; preparing to answer questions about products and services

Computer literacy: Having basic computer skills to enhance access to leads and to relevant financial, market, and competitive data; being aware of and understanding the resources available and being able to use them to improve sales

Competition: Having basic knowledge of key competitors and being aware of how the company's products compare with competitors'

Personality

Sociability: Desire to interact with others and to project warmth and relate well to a wide variety of people

Self-sufficiency/self-motivation: Ability to work independently for extended periods of time with minimal support and approval, to take initiative, be proactive, and take ownership for personal success

High energy level: Has a strong work ethic; is able to maintain a fast pace while staying focused in stressful situations

Competitiveness: Demonstrates the desire to achieve and surpass goals, work with persistence in the face of obstacles, and thrive in high-pressure situations

Self-confidence: Believes in their own abilities; approaches work with the expectation of success and an awareness of what is required for success; accepts criticism constructively and is willing to admit mistakes without blaming others

Reliability/trustworthiness: Behaves consistently and predictably; is dependable in all phases of the sales process; is able to gain the trust of the customer by being honest, working with integrity, and meeting commitments

Ethics: Has high professional and personal standards, treats people fairly and with respect, provides a straightforward discussion of price and payment issues, and is honest in all communications; refrains from being manipulative or obscuring facts

Ability

Mental agility: Flexible enough to deal with multiple issues at the same time, able to maintain a constantly high level of alertness, and possesses a broad learning capacity

Analytical skills: Ability to reason with, analyze, and draw conclusions from facts and data

Empathy: Understands and displays sensitivity to customer needs and concerns and minimizes customer anxiety and frustration

Openness: Is eager to consider new ideas and available to learn new things; is comfortable with change and ambiguity and open to a variety of options to meet the customer's needs

References

Boyatzis, R. E. *The Competent Manager: A Model for Effective Performance.* New York: Wiley, 1982.

Briscoe, J. P. *Competency-Based Approaches to Selecting and Developing Executives: Current Practices and Suggestions for Improvement.* Boston: Executive Development Roundtable, Boston University, 1996.

Davis, R. S., and Olson, D. A. "Leverage Training and Development to Make a Strategic Impact." *The Journal* (Society of Insurance Trainers and Educators), 1996–1997, pp. 10–12.

Dubois, D. *Competency-Based Performance Improvement: A Strategy for Organizational Change.* Amherst, Mass.: HRD Press, 1993.

Dubois, D. *The Competency Case Book.* Amherst, Mass.: HRD Press, 1998.

Eubanks, J. L., Marshall, J. B., and O'Driscoll, M. P. "A Competency Model for OD Practitioners." *Training & Development Journal,* Nov. 1990, pp. 85–90.

Flanagan, J. C. "The Critical Incident Technique." *Psychological Bulletin,* 1954, 51(4), 327–358.

Goleman, D. "The New Competency Tests: Matching the Right People to the Right Jobs." *Psychology Today,* Jan. 1981, pp. 35–44.

Holdeman, J. B., Aldridge, J. M., and Jackson, D. "How to Hire Ms./Mr. Right." *Journal of Accountancy,* Aug. 1996, pp. 55–57.

Horney, N. F., and Koonce, R. "The Missing Piece in Reengineering." *Training & Development,* Dec. 1995, pp. 37–43.

Klemp, G. O. (Ed.) *The Assessment of Occupational Competence.* Washington, D.C.: Report to the National Institute of Education, 1980.

Lepsinger, R., and Lucia, A. *The Art and Science of 360° Feedback.* San Francisco: Jossey-Bass/Pfeiffer, 1997.

Linkage, Inc. *Introduction to Competency Modeling.* Lexington, Mass.: Linkage, 1997.

Lombardo, M. M., and Eichinger, R. W. *For Your Improvement: A Development and Coaching Guide.* Minneapolis, Minn.: Lominger Limited, 1996.

Mansfield, R. S. "Building Competency Models: Approaches for HR Professionals." *Human Resource Management,* 1996, 35(1), 7–18.

Manus and MOHR. *Sales Competencies for the Twenty-First Century.* Report published using research conducted by Manus and MOHR. Stamford/Ridgefield, Conn.: Manus and MOHR, 1997.

McCall, M. W., Lombardo, M. M., and Morrison, A. M. *The Lessons of Experience: How Successful Executives Develop on the Job.* Lexington, Mass.: Heath, 1988.

McClelland, D. C. "Testing for Competence Rather than for 'Intelligence.'" *American Psychologist*, 1973, 28(1), 1–14.

McIlvaine, A. R. "World Premiere." *Human Resource Executive*, Oct. 19, 1998, pp. 18–20.

McLagan, P. A. "Competencies: The Next Generation." *Training & Development Journal*, May 1997, pp. 40–47.

McLagan, P. A. "The Models." *Models for HRD Practice.* Alexandria, Va..: American Society for Training and Development, 1989.

O'Neill, C. P. "Competencies—A Powerful Tool for Driving Business Results." *Human Resource Professional*, Nov.–Dec. 1996, pp. 22–24.

Parry, S. R. "The Quest for Competencies." *Training*, July 1996, pp. 48–56

Personnel Decisions International. *Successful Manager's Handbook: Development Suggestions for Today's Managers.* USA: Personnel Decisions International, 1996.

Raelin, J. A., and Cooledge, A. S. "From Generic to Organic Competencies." *Human Resource Planning*, Spring 1996, pp. 24–33.

Rollins, T., and Fruge, M. "Performance Dimensions: Competencies with a Twist." *Training*, Jan. 1992, pp. 47–51.

Rothwell, W. J. *Beyond Training and Development: State-of-the-Art Strategies for Enhancing Human Performance.* New York: AMACOM, 1996.

Rothwell, W. J., Prescott, R. K., and Taylor, M. W. *Strategic Human Resource Leader: How to Prepare Your Organization for the Six Key Trends Shaping the Future.* Palo Alto, Calif.: Davies-Black, 1998.

Spangenberg, H. *Assessing Managerial Competence.* Kenwyn: Juta, 1990.

Spencer, L. M., and Spencer, S. M. *Competence at Work: Models for Superior Performance.* New York: Wiley, 1993.

Welkowitz, J., Ewen, R. B., and Cohen, J. *Introductory Statistics for the Behavioral Sciences.* (3rd. ed.) Orlando: Academic Press, 1982.

Zemke, R., and Kramlinger, T. *Figuring Things Out: A Trainer's Guide to Needs and Task Analysis.* Reading, Mass.: Addison-Wesley, 1982.

The Authors

ANNTOINETTE D. (TONI) LUCIA is a managing partner of Manus, a Right Management Consultants company that specializes in helping organizations implement business strategies successfully. Her consulting work has included facilitating organizational change; team building for senior management teams; linking human resource plans to strategic plans; ensuring the successful integration of teams following mergers; designing, conducting, and evaluating executive and management development programs; developing competency models; and using feedback systems to help individual executives improve their effectiveness. Lucia has recently served as a consultant for Alliant Foodservice, Chase Manhattan Bank, General Electric, the Geon Company, Household International, J. P. Morgan, KPMG Peat Marwick, Lehman Brothers, the New York Stock Exchange, PaineWebber, Pfizer, and Subaru of America. She was also a consultant for GE's Work-Out! and Change Acceleration Process. She designed a program for the Center for Creative Leadership that focuses on career and professional development planning for high-potential managers. She also serves on the Board of Directors of ISA.

RICHARD (RICK) LEPSINGER is a managing partner of Manus, a Right Management Consultants company that specializes in helping organizations implement business strategies successfully. He has been a consultant in management and organization for more that twenty years, including serving as consultant for managers and management teams at Coca-Cola, Allied Signal, KPMG Peat Marwick, Lehman Brothers, the New York Stock Exchange, Prudential,

PaineWebber, Subaru of America, Bayer Pharmaceuticals, Pfizer, and Union Carbide, among others. Lepsinger has extensive experience in formulating and implementing strategic plans and in developing and using feedback-based technology to help organizations and managers identify their strengths and weaknesses. He has addressed executive conferences and made presentations on strategic leadership, strategy formulation, 360-degree feedback and its uses, and developing and using competency models to enhance organizational effectiveness. He has worked with large-scale management simulations as part of assessment and training interventions since 1979.

Index

Page numbers in *italics* reference Exhibit titles and topics, and sample documents.

A

Academic training, 129, 131

Accelerated Competency Systems Method, 19

Action plan, competency models development, 56, *56–63*; accountability assignments, *57–59*; addressing causes of resistance, *159–161*; communication channels, 61; potential problems probability and impact, 59–61, *62*; resource requirements, *57–59*, 153, *160*; schedule, *57–59*. *See also* Competency models development

Action Planning Worksheet, *58–59*

Advancement, career. *See* Succession planning system, HRM

Advocacy. *See* Commitment to using competency models

Agenda: "day-in-the-life" observation, *78–79*; focus group, 77

Aldinger, B., 44

Aldridge, J. M., 24

Analysis of data. *See* Data collection and analysis; Statistical analysis

Appraisal system. *See* Performance appraisal and management system, HRM

ARCO Transportation, 11

The Art and Science of 360° Feedback (Lepsinger and Lucia), 129

Attendance problems, interview and focus group, *62*

B

Baca, M., 39, 41–42

Behaviors: 360-degree feedback questionnaire based on, *127–128*; competencies with a range of observable, *134–135*; in the Competency Pyramid, 6–7; core competency, 8, 41, 154, 157; examples for each competency, 124–125, *126*; interviews and focus groups questions on, *72–73*; and performance success, 9; predictive principles for, 119–120; probing for specific, 75–76; specificity and job applicability of, 141; succession planning candidate evaluation, 138, *139*; supporting organizational values, 14, 154–155; two ways to describe competency, 132–136. *See also* Performance observation

"Bench strength." *See* Succession planning system, HRM

Benefits of Competency Models in HRM Systems, *23*

Berlew, D., 18

Bias, avoidance of, 30, 89, 90, 155

Bosses. *See* Managers

Boundaryless organization concept, 42

Boyatzis, R. E., 49

Briscoe, J. P., 21

Brooklyn Union Gas, 39–42

Business needs addressed by competency models, 9–14, 51–52; adapting to change, 12–13, 150, 154–155; aligning behavior with organizational strategies and values, 13–14, 155; clarifying job and work expectations, 9–10, 150–151, 155–156 157; consistent standards, 10; in context, 64, 82–83, 85, 101–103; examples of, 2, *3–4*, 52; focusing on, 86, 153, *159*; hiring the best available people, 10–11, 41, 115, 119–120; managing

.